J Hughes
July 2005

the post-evangelical

foreword by
dallas willard

the
post
evangelical

dave
tomlinson

revised north american edition

www.emergentys.com

WWW.ZONDERVAN.COM

The Post-Evangelical (Revised North American Edition)

Copyright © 2003 by Dave Tomlinson

emergentYS Books, 300 South Pierce Street, El Cajon, CA 92020 are published by Zondervan, 5300 Patterson Avenue Southeast, Grand Rapids, MI 49530.

Library of Congress Cataloging-in-Publication Data

Tomlinson, Dave.
  The post-evangelical / by Dave Tomlinson.
     p. cm.
Includes bibliographical references (p. 141-146).
  ISBN 0-310-25385-3 (pbk.)
  1. Postmodernism--Religious aspects--Christianity. 2.
Evangelicalism. I. Title.
  BR115.P74T66 2003
  230'.04624--dc21

                                                          2002156594

Web site addresses listed in this book were current at the time of publication. Please contact Youth Specialties via e-mail (YS@YouthSpecialties.com) to report URLs that are no longer operational and replacement URLs if available.

Edited by John Suk
Cover and interior design by c.a.n. design
Additional writing by Joseph R. Myers

(Originally published in Great Britain in 1995 by Triangle, Society for Promoting Christian Knowledge, Holy Trinity Church, Marylebone Road, London NW 1 4DU.)

Printed in the United States of America

03 04 05 06 07/ DC / 10 9 8 7 6 5 4 3 2 1

Dedicated to Steve Fairnie, a true post-evangelical,
who left us much too soon.

about the contributors

Timothy Keel is the founding pastor of Jacob's Well Church in Kansas City, Missouri. He received his Master of Divinity degree from Denver Seminary and Bachelor of Fine Arts degree from the University of Kansas. Tim is married to Mimi and the father of Mabry, Annelise, and Blaise. His interests include monastic life and culture, reading, writing, and all things Middle-Earth.

Mark Galli is managing editor of *Christianity Today*. He has been an editor at *Leadership* and *Christian History* and has written books on preaching, prayer, ministry, and church history, his most recent being *Francis Assisi and His World* (Lion, 2002). He is a member of St. Mark's Episcopal Church in Glen Ellyn, Illinois.

Joseph R. Myers is the author of *The Search to Belong: Rethinking Intimacy, Community, and Small Groups*, also published by emergentYS. He owns the consulting firm, FrontPorch, which helps churches, business, and other organizations promote and develop healthy community. He's also founding partner—with his wife, Sara—of settingPace, a communication arts group based in Cincinnati.

Doug Pagitt is senior pastor of Solomon's Porch in Minneapolis, Minnesota. Formerly he was director of the Young Leader Networks for Leadership Network and a staff pastor at Wooddale Church in Eden Prarie, Minnesota. Doug is also a senior fellow of Emergent.

Holly Rankin Zaher is currently the Visiting Professor for Youth Ministry at Trinity Episcopal School for Ministry (www.tesm.edu) and the Assistant Director for Professional Training at Rock the World Youth Mission Alliance (www.rocktheworld.org). Being a part of the Emergent Coordinating Group (www.emergentvillage.org), crocheting, and trying to learn how to remember movie quotes consumes most of her life. Holly lives in Kittanning, Pennsylvania, with her husband, Jim.

A philosophy professor at U.S.C., **Dallas Willard** is author of *The Divine Conspiracy: Rediscovering Our Hidden Life in God* (HarperCollins, 1998), voted *Christianity Today's* Book of the Year. It's the second in a three-part series that includes *Hearing From God: Developing a Conversational Relationship with God* (InterVarsity Press, 1999) and *The Spirit of the Disciplines* (HarperCollins, 1988). His newest book is *Renovation of the Heart* (NavPress, 2002).

Owner of Youth Specialties, **Mike Yaconelli** is a popular speaker the world over. He pastors a small church in Yreka, California, with his wife, Karla. His latest books are *Messy Spirituality: Spirituality for the Rest of Us* (Zondervan) and *Dangerous Wonder: The Adventure of Childlike Faith* (NavPress).

contents

smothering

jesus in a heap

of trivialities

a foreword by dallas willard

smothering jesus in a heap of trivialities

Dave Tomlinson addresses a group of serious contemporary problems for a large segment of the church in *The Post-Evangelical,* problems that consist of issues much deeper and broader than this book title suggests. They are problems that have a very special significance for what is now called evangelicalism—especially since evangelicalism is basking in its historical day in the sun.

To correctly appreciate this, you have to start with the realization that what Tomlinson calls *post*-evangelicalism is by no means *ex*-evangelicalism. There are, of course ex-evangelicals, and even anti-evangelicals, but post-evangelicals *are* evangelicals, perhaps tenaciously so. However, post-evangelicals have also been driven to the margins by some aspects of evangelical church culture with which they cannot honestly identify.

The inner conflict post-evangelicals experience is usually rooted in a simple but devastating situation, one that Old Testament prophets often inveighed against. In this situation, the details of what is "only right and proper" to achieve social acceptance within the evangelical group increasingly focus upon things that have little to do with the heart of evangelical faith, or even run counter to it. However, these details are treated as basic, or at least highly desirable, if one wishes to maintain status as an "acceptable" evangelical Christian.

Thus, in Jesus' day, there were people who painstakingly gave a tithe of one seed in ten from their herb garden, and yet disregarded justice and the love of God. They replaced, probably without even realizing it, the genuine commandments of God with the traditions of human beings. Tragically, this kind of incongruity drives people—who will never be anything but evangelical in their deepest beliefs—to the margins or out the doors of the evangelical church.

While our secular culture may have some influence on the move toward a post-evangelical posture, most of the motivation in that direction, as I have observed it through the years, is from *within* evangelical teaching and experience. This is due to an inherent tension that has always existed within the evangelical tradition. On one hand, it emphasizes as essential a personal, life-transforming *experience* of God. The one thing that has always been distinctive to evangelical Christianity is its rejection of second-hand faith, mediated through institutions of which one is a member. On the other hand, the evangelical tradition takes the

the post-evangelical

certain interpretations of the Bible, or certain biblical texts, as ultimate authority on what is to be believed and practiced. These two elements of evangelical Christianity are in constant tension.

St. Francis of Assisi and Martin Luther are fascinating case studies of how the tension between experience and authority works. In their cases, authority won out. In fact, anytime a significant social group or institution develops around a teaching or an individual, authority typically wins out. For then the question isn't *Where are you before God?* It's rather, *Are you a member of our group? (Are you really?)* Those responsible for the integrity of the group usually see to it that the marks of group membership are endorsed by the authority source—in our case, a set of interpretations about the Bible. So for example, issues such as whether you believe that women should be allowed to teach or whether Christ will return soon after the millennium begins may be used as tests for whether or not you believe the Bible—and that test, in turn, may be used as a test of whether you are evangelical (or was that "Christian"?). And so on. The vital relationship to Jesus is smothered in a heap of trivialities.

And what, at that point, has become of the other wing of the evangelical tension? What has become of the ongoing walk with Jesus Christ and the integrity of soul that permits one to worship the Father in Spirit and in truth? The sad truth is that you can be an evangelical in excellent standing without these experiences! Certainly the folks who fit the term *post-evangelical* are not right about everything, but here they are on to something of extreme importance to anyone concerned about the cause of Christ and the welfare of human beings today.

Those of us who hold dear the evangelical form of Christian faith must come to grips with these issues. We shouldn't spend too much time worrying about the failures of other forms of religion, Christian or not. We must accept that the house of God—where judgment begins—is *our* house. In North America, especially, the evangelical form of Christian faith has achieved remarkable acceptance and prominence in recent decades. But we have not done well in four absolutely crucial areas:

- We haven't figured out what the spiritual life is really like, inside and out.
- We haven't dealt successfully with the challenge of transfoming our characters into routine Christlikeness.
- We haven't succeeded in transforming our workplaces and

vocations into extensions of the kingdom of Christ.

• We haven't learned how to live in God's power in every aspect of our lives. "Whatever you do in word or deed," as Paul told us, "do all in the name of [on behalf of, in the power of] the Lord Jesus, giving thanks to God the Father through him" (Colossians 3:17) How do evangelicals do that?

The post-evangelicals among us—and they are among us, in large numbers—are for the most part those who, *because* of their evangelical insights or suspicions, cannot accept a *form* of evangelical religious culture that makes the heart of evangelical faith irrelevant and the heart of the prophetic biblical tradition anything but subversive. We need to listen to them openly and carefully as we continue to study our Bibles and seek to hear from God.

—*Dallas Willard*

introduction

introduction

> We have a choice between two attitudes toward the future...one of
> imagination, the other of nostalgia...it's a choice between *facing* the
> future, and *backing into* it.[1]
>
> —Stephen Toulmin

This book arose from a chance conversation in the summer of 1993. I
was at Greenbelt, an annual Christian arts festival in the south of
England, leading a series of seminars. Late one evening a few of us were
winding down and chewing over the day's events when one of my
friends made a passing reference to "we post-evangelicals," quickly followed by, "whatever that means."

The conversation moved on and eventually we went to bed. But
the implied question continued rattling around my brain: *What is a post-
evangelical?* The term must have entered our consciousness surrepti-
tiously two or three years earlier, but no one had ever explained it. The
next day I awoke with a determination to do just that. My book, *The Post-
Evangelical*, was published in the U.K. two years later, just in time for the
1995 Greenbelt Festival.

The decision to release the book in time for Greenbelt was delib-
erate. The festival is a gathering place for Christians with the kinds of
questions that are often difficult to ask in churches. If the book had an
audience, Greenbelt would be as good a place as any to find it.

The decision was justified. Halfway through the weekend, stocks
of the book were completely sold out, and the bookshop manager
reported it to be the fastest-selling book in his seven years at the festival. Meanwhile, a thousand or so people packed my seminar tent, with
many more outside. *The Church Times* printed a photograph of the over-
flow crowd peering into the marquee, with the teasing caption: "Outside
the fold, but still looking in."

Needless to say, the book had its detractors, even at Greenbelt.
Throughout the weekend a dedicated group of hecklers stalked me,
determined to shout down my "heresies." Still the book's overall reception suggests that its content resonated with an impulse felt by many
evangelicals at the start of the twenty-first century. The book is, in fact, a
pastoral essay directed at those who experience this impulse, people
who struggle with restrictions in evangelical theology, spirituality, and
church culture—yet who still desire to pursue their faith journey.

the post-evangelical

The post-evangelical impulse does not necessarily imply a move away from Christian orthodoxy or evangelical faith. Rather it demonstrates that to remain true to a tradition, we must come to terms with its changing cultural context in order to find an authentic expression of that tradition—"you have to change to stay the same."[2] Yet experiencing change can be uncomfortable and confusing. A friend suggested that post-evangelicals may sometimes share the experience of Topsy in *Uncle Tom's Cabin*: "How can I know what I mean until I hear what I say?"[3] This book is an attempt to articulate the experience, thoughts, and feelings of post-evangelicals, as well as to help them understand, refine, and critique their experiences.

In the months that followed the publication of *The Post-Evangelical*, virtually every Christian magazine and newspaper in Britain reviewed it, and their responses were sharply divided. Nick Mercer, former assistant principal of London Bible College, wrote: "This is a long overdue book which springs out of a growing concern many of us have within evangelicalism—about the large numbers of nomadic ex-evangelicals, about the cultural and theological constraints that seem to be part and parcel of British evangelicalism, about the relief many voice when you dare to express doubt and agnosticism in public meetings, about brain-dead emotionalism."[4]

On the other hand, Alister McGrath, a leading evangelical theologian, branded the book as "one of the most superficial and inadequate treatments of the contemporary state of evangelicalism" he had read.[5] As an admirer of Alister McGrath, I was disappointed by his response, especially since he failed to engage with anything I actually wrote. Along with certain other evangelical leaders, he dismissed the arguments out of hand, giving the impression that this thing needed stamping out before it took hold.

But the vast majority of reviewers—even those who disagreed with my conclusions—acknowledged that the book highlighted problems within British evangelicalism. Many recognised the post-evangelical impulse within churches. One conservative writer went so far as to admit: "The weaknesses Tomlinson identifies in evangelicalism are genuine, and there is a potentially large constituency of Evangelicals who, without reading his book, may nevertheless soon seize on its title to describe their own position."[6]

introduction

This last observation proved especially apt nine months after the publication of *The Post-Evangelical*, when *Third Way*, a thoughtful evangelical magazine, announced that, in a survey, 24 percent of their readers now identified themselves as post-evangelical. Now, nine years later, many people do customarily refer to themselves as "post-evangelical," whether or not they have read the book, or even heard of it.

Yet for me, the most satisfying indicator that my message had struck a chord lay in the hundreds of letters and e-mails I received—and continue to receive. They revealed that the receptive audience was far broader than originally anticipated. I wrote the book for disaffected evangelicals in their twenties or early thirties (Generation Xers), whose general outlook and attitudes were significantly influenced by post-modern culture. Yet much of the correspondence came from older and more culturally conservative people. Even though they probably looked like "satisfied customers" in their churches, they also clearly harboured a raft of doubts and questions.

After a short time I could predict what most letters would say before opening them. The overwhelming reaction was one of relief:

"At last someone has said it."

"Thank God I'm not alone."

"I've thought some of these things for years, but I didn't dare say."

"Great relief and a regaining of confidence have followed the reading of your book. So I'm not mad after all."

The letters told stories about the struggles people experienced trying to make sense of their faith in churches not always comfortable with their questions. Some talked about intellectual tussles with doctrines they couldn't swallow, others of longings for a deeper spirituality. Some were frustrated at the lack of social and political engagement in their churches, others cringed at self-righteous moralizing. Most found the evangelical subculture insular, self-congratulatory, and often, embarrassing.

Many of the letters I received also voiced exasperation at the sense of certainty and hype experienced in some evangelical churches, where they found it particularly hard to express disquiet or to question prevailing attitudes. Indeed, I contend that the fundamentalist tone in

the post-evangelical

much charismatic theology fuels the post-evangelical impulse. A color-ful letter from a university professor powerfully sums up what many people feel:

> *A year ago I was in a state of rage bordering on church burning. I felt like Winston having escaped from Big Brother or the savage in Brave New World, and wanted revenge for all those sermons, miserable-worm guilt feelings, and the ludicrous new-speak that had been my life for twenty years. There was no church I could go into without having a severe reaction and either walking out or putting my fin-gers in my ears and going "la la la la"—which my wife found embar-rassing and looked like demonization to those who are so wise about these things.*
>
> *A copy of your book was the first hint that I was not entirely alone. I am now completely free from that stifling kind of religion that slowly strangles the life out of you and from the susceptibility to completely flee reality. My spirituality is now my own, not an undi-gested mixture interjected from a thousand grim sermons and silly books. I can get in touch with the strength of it, deep inside. I can read the words of Jesus, but their meaning has now changed like rain into snowflakes. My mind is now open and not tight shut, and I feel an almost primitive sense of freedom and energy.*

Now, all evangelical churches are not the same. Some are much more open-minded than others. However, the widespread nature of the post-evangelical impulse suggests that it is much more than just a reac-tion against extreme fundamentalism. My travels around the world have also convinced me that this is not just a British phenomenon, as some have suggested. Wherever there are evangelicals (in the Western world, at least), there are post-evangelicals, whether or not they adopt that label.

I am very pleased, therefore, to see a North American edition of *The Post-Evangelical*, and I am grateful to Youth Specialties and church leaders of Emergent for making it happen. America and Britain share an enormous amount in common, but regular visits across the pond have

introduction

taught me that our religious situations are far from identical. So I appreciate Joseph R. Myers replacing my original whistle-stop tour of recent developments in British evangelicalism with an equivalent American version. Myers' chapter helps me understand how the post-evangelical impulse took root on this side of the Atlantic.

But I think we can go further. Conversation with people in other church traditions convince me that a similar impulse exists in other parts of the church, too. Indeed, people have told me that even though their faith journeys differ from those in the evangelical camp, they find themselves traveling the same road, perhaps as "post-Catholics" or "post-liberals," for example.

We shouldn't be surprised that an impulse similar to post-evangelicalism is shared in different ways by people around the world and in different sections of the Church. The changes we evangelicals are experiencing are linked, after all, to a wider cultural shift in Western societies.

The notion that our broader cultural context shapes how evangelicals and all other Christians "do" church will be highly suspect for many evangelicals. They believe that the message of Christ must be, and can be, protected from cultural entanglements.

But I am advocating critical engagement with the wider culture, not unthinking absorption into it. Since his death and resurrection, the meaning of Jesus Christ for his followers has been illuminated by many different cultural and philosophical perspectives—including, most recently, the methods and insights of modernity. Christians must engage contemporary culture if they wish to know how to make the good news of Jesus relevant to people in that culture. By engaging critically, Christians will also identify those elements in postmodern culture (e.g., hedonism) that run counter to the claims of Christ.

The Post-Evangelical should be seen as the beginning of a journey, not the end. While it appears on the reading lists of various college and university courses, it makes no claim to be an academic work or alternative systematic theology. Much more work is needed to develop post-evangelical themes, and I am pleased by the number of research projects this book has already provoked. More importantly, as I have already stressed, the book comes from a pastoral concern. I hope it empowers ordinary people with the confidence to think for themselves as they explore the breadth of the Christian community, now in North America as well as in Britain and Europe. (Incidentally, I am now the vicar of St. Luke's Church, Holloway, in North London, which attempts to work out the principles behind Holy Joe's in a more regular church setting. Due to time constraints, I am no longer able to be involved with Holy Joe's on a regular basis.)

— *Dave Tomlinson, Vicar of St. Luke's Church,*
  Holloway, North London
  October 2002

01

a symbol of
hope

a symbol of hope

Talking about the "post-evangelical" may seem strange when others are talking about an evangelical renaissance. Yet the subject is of vital concern to an increasing number of people who feel the urge to explore new possibilities with regard to their faith. It's also surprising how many people who hear the term *post-evangelical* for the first time immediately understand its significance and have a rough idea what it might imply, even when they're not formally trained in theology. In fact, for many of them, the term "post-evangelical" has become a welcome rallying point, a symbol of hope.

Why people need such a hope, and what they might find is this book's topic. I should begin, however, with a bit of background. Although I talked extensively to many people with different viewpoints about this book's subject matter, I have not set out to present a survey of their opinions. Also, I'm not writing as a dispassionate onlooker. I consider myself post-evangelical.

The book operates on three levels. First, *The Post-Evangelical* is an apologetic, an explanation of an important trend in evangelicalism. Second, it's a pastoral response to those who feel confused as to where they stand vis-à-vis contemporary evangelicalism. I suggest that they are probably not alone in thinking and feeling as they do. And third, this book discusses some of the thorny issues, and offers alternative interpretations, for people struggling with evangelicalism-as-usual. I believe the lack of ready alternatives to evangelicalism-as-usual is a major reason why people give up the quest altogether, and consequently become ex-Christians.**(a)**

A man I met at a garden party comes to mind. After a brief conversation, he confessed that he

> **(a)** One widely held assumption is that people are not attracted to the faith, or give up on faith, because of the way evangelicals think about and practice their faith. This is no doubt true in some cases, but we should take more seriously the idea that the gospel is inherently an offense "to Jews and Greeks," that is, to all manner of people. It seems most postmoderns—like most people in general—reject the gospel because they don't want to submit to its demands, not because it's presented in a "modern" way.
> **—Mark Galli**

had once been an evangelical Christian, but now considered himself an agnostic. On hearing more of his story, it sounded to me as if his problems had more to do with the dogmatic strand of evangelicalism he had encountered than with God. I told him this, and we talked for a long time about the difficulties that had finally led him to throw in the towel. He was a thinking person who could not accept things simply because he was told that they were so, and unfortunately this is exactly what had been expected of him. If there had been space for him to explore ideas for himself—albeit with guidance and care from others—I believe his story could have turned out quite differently. Thankfully, he has now found that space and is rediscovering a way forward within the Christian faith.

Why "Post"-Evangelical?

Most people who contemplate the possibilities of being "post"-evangelical do so because of the difficulty they have reconciling what they see and experience in evangelicalism with their own values, theological reflection and intuition. For some people the agony created by this conflict is considerable.**(b)**

(b) Evangelicals want to know "can I live this way?" Much of my own personal and pastoral experience suggests that people struggle hard to live within the tensions that Dave describes. Most people try to ignore the dissonance they feel, or they give up on church altogether. There's no obvious third option, and the hidden barb is that no one talks about the struggle until it's too late. It seems ironic that a group of people who value "truth" so highly struggle so much with something as simple as honesty.
—Timothy Keel

For example, one young man, who had grown up in an evangelical home, spoke to me of the pain of his dilemma: "I don't know where to go. I no longer feel I can call myself an evangelical, yet I certainly don't wish to be a liberal. What am I?" Others are more nonchalant about it, like the young woman who said, "Evangelicalism helped me to begin with, but I feel I've outgrown it now." Arrogant? Possibly. Yet she voiced something that cropped up continually in my discussions with people—the feeling that while evangelicalism is supremely good at introducing people to faith in Christ, it's distinctly unhelpful when it comes to encouraging a more "grown up" experience of faith.**(c)**

(c) One morning during the early days of our church planting experience, some of us gathered to share our faith journeys. We noticed that after the initial rush of our "come to Jesus/salvation prayer" moments, we missed ongoing connections to others who were invested in discipling us rather than merely converting us as part of evangelistic programs. These conversions are like births without parenting—as if once the uterus is empty, the relationship ends. I contend that some people become post-evangelical because evangelicalism values "birthing" newborn souls above the care and feeding of them. Unfortunately, abandoned newborns die.
—Timothy Keel

What does *grown up* mean?**(d)** Lots of things, so I will just mention the one definition I heard cited most often: the desire to interact on a more positive level with non-evangelical theologies and perspectives.

a symbol of hope

By that definition, I mean "post"–evangelicals—potential or actual—often perceive that alternative perspectives are mentioned in evangelical circles only to promptly dismiss them as rubbish or disgraceful compromises. Let me illustrate this point with an analogy. Being a frequent traveler up and down the interstates, I often scan the radio for something interesting to listen to. Doing so, I'm always amazed at the different ways various stations report the same news item. Sometimes I even wonder if I'm hearing about the same event. The contrast between stations becomes even greater if I listen to reports about the same incident from overseas stations. And if I *really* want to be confused, I listen to commentators, who seem able to produce diametrically opposing views on virtually every subject!**(e)**

Post-evangelicals have tired of listening only to the evangelical networks, so they have tuned in to other stations, too. As they listen to new and diverse interpretations of the Christian faith, they find that initial confusion soon gives way to exhilaration. For them, a more "grown up" environment is one in which there are fewer predigested opinions, fewer categorical conclusions, and a lot more space to explore alternative ideas.**(f)** Post-evangelicals also want room to express doubt without having someone rush around in a mad panic trying to "deliver" them from unbelief. Far too often doubt is portrayed simply as an enemy rather

(d) In her book **Beyond Liberalism and Fundamentalism**, Nancey Murphy writes that modern culture created the polarities of liberalism and fundamentalism (or, I would add, conservativism and evangelicalism). I would argue that since the modern culture created these two polar opposites—and since we are entering into a new culture—another way of viewing Christianity is needed. I'm not sure I agree with Dave here. Is being a "post-evangelical" really about one "growing out" of evangelicalism? I would say that a new way of looking at Christianity is needed because of our current culture shift and not because of a change in maturity.
—**Holly Rankin Zaher**

(e) Christian (that is, evangelical) radio is a good case study for this phenomenon. Such radio seems obsessed with two subjects: personal salvation and harping on how popular culture has abandoned Judeo-Christian values. The culture war is part of our evangelical genetic code. If so, Dave's hope for a "grown up" expression of faith stemming from evangelicalism may well come up short.
—**Timothy Keel**

(f) Faith is more than an intellectual buffet where we are given permission to try this or that. Faith is a relationship with Jesus complete with all the twists and turns that relationships bring. It's in the tussle of following this Jesus—during the process of getting to know God—that I am surprised, confronted, exposed, challenged, and pushed beyond my comfort zone. The word for this dynamic interaction with God is **growth**. Not only does my faith in Christ allow me more space to explore alternative ideas, my faith allows me the space to follow Jesus wherever he goes. I wish Dave would have argued that many of us have no choice about this; if we want to follow Jesus, and we do, then we must go where he goes, ignoring, as we should, those who say we can't go there.
—**Mike Yaconelli**

than a potential friend; as something mature Christians should not suffer from, rather than a vital means by which Christians mature.

In this environment, post-evangelicals are tempted to up and leave the evangelical tradition and move elsewhere. For some this may be a good decision. But it would be a great mistake to imagine that what we're discussing is a mere "tempest in the evangelical teacup." Narrow-mindedness and dogmatism are to be found in churches of all traditions. In other Christian traditions, the theological questions may not be the same, but the feeling of social claustrophobia can be, as was demonstrated by a television documentary made by Karen Armstrong, the author and former nun. The similarity between what Catholics were saying to her about the Roman Catholic Church and what post-evangelicals say about evangelical churches was quite extraordinary. The same issues arise in other traditions. Even liberals can be dogmatically liberal! All in all, swapping traditions is not necessarily a solution to the questions post-evangelicals are asking.

There is a final difficulty with switching churches. When the chips are down, disillusioned evangelicals often discover that their evangelical background still counts for something. At this point, it might be helpful to give a brief explanation of the term *evangelical*.

What Do We Mean by "Evangelical"?

The term "evangelical" has been prominent in at least three earlier periods of Protestant history.[1] Although the term itself derives from the Greek word *euangelion*, meaning "gospel" or "good news," its present use dates back to the Reformation, when it described the emerging Protestant movement, and especially the Lutheran wing of the movement. During the eighteenth and nineteenth century era of evangelical revivals, the term was associated with the likes of Wesley, Moody, and Finny. More recently, the late nineteenth and early twentieth centuries were the period of evangelical fundamentalism. Each of these periods contributed substantially to the character of present-day evangelicalism. The Reformation established the supremacy of biblical authority over the authorities of both the Pope and church tradition; it also gave prominence to the doctrine of justification by faith. The emphasis of the evangelical revivals was on personal conversion, holiness of life, and the need to preach the gospel. The fundamentalist period was characterized by

a symbol of hope

the defense of the Bible in the face of perceived attacks from science, history, and modernist theology.

Although one writer has described no fewer than 16 distinct strands of evangelicalism,[2] we can, even from this simple historical outline, identify several major features common to most evangelicals across the denominational spectrum. Evangelicals recognize faith in Christ's atoning work as absolutely central. They assert that this faith must be personal, leading to an experience of conversion. They stress the importance of declaring the gospel to non-believers. They hold to the supremacy of Scripture over all other sources of authority. Some, like the fundamentalists, claim that the Bible is inerrant, (the belief that in its original form it contained no errors or mistakes), and most hold a position very close to inerrancy even though they do not like the word. Evangelicals also universally believe in the actual, historical nature of events like the virgin birth, the miracles, and the death and bodily resurrection of Christ.**(g)**

> **(9)** Though Dave recognizes variety in evangelicalism, here he paints the movement in broad brushstrokes. But evangelicalism today really is diverse in terms of belief, practice, and social structure—there is a world of difference between Tony Campolo and James Dobson, for example, yet both are "evangelicals." In short, it's no longer possible to generalize about the movement. These criticisms are more representative of the fundamentalist wing than evangelicalism as a whole. The "post-evangelicalism" championed in these pages could more accurately be described as "post-fundamentalism" or "post-legalism."
> **—Mark Galli**

It would be quite misleading, however, to describe evangelicalism simply in terms of beliefs. Evangelicalism must also be understood as a "culture" with a particular social ambience. When a person becomes an evangelical Christian, he or she enters subculture with its own church services, festivals, concerts, conferences, magazines, books, merchandise, record companies, mission organizations, training schemes, vacation clubs, and celebrities. They will also encounter distinctive social attitudes and behavioral expectations, which at best might be interpreted as the right way for Christians to live, and at worst are criticized as being christianized, middle-class conservatism. To be fair, evangelicalism is probably a mixture of both.

The bottom line is that upon entering this strange, new world of evangelicalism individuals are expected to change, and generally *do*. How much of this change stems from the Holy Spirit recreating the individual in the image of Christ, and how much change stems from the pressure of a social situation squeezing someone into the mold of evan-

the post-evangelical

(h) Evangelical culture is a ghetto inaccessible to all but evangelicals. While at first glance the ghetto suggests evangelicals are "in the world, but not of it," they have merely co-opted secular-speak into God-talk: "God's Gym" for "Gold's Gym," "This Blood's for You" for "This Bud's for You" on T-shirts, and "Testamint" breath mints (always an opportunity to witness). Tragically, life in this ghetto fails to address the larger issues of Western, consumptive materialism; worse, it thrives on the "trinket-ization" and trivialization of Christianity.
—Timothy Keel

(i) Dave has named what the real issue is in evangelicalism—power. Evangelicals are enamored with power and control. That's why numbers and measures are so important to evangelicals, and why compliance is next to godliness. What's important to evangelicals is freeing you from the world that squeezes you into its mold so evangelicalism can, in turn, squeeze you into **its** mold. Evangelicals resist and declare as enemy anything they can't control—including God, by the way. A post-evangelical is not a one-time evangelical who's given up on truth, she's an evangelical who's given up on control.
—**Mike Yaconelli**

gelical culture is a matter of judgment.**(h,i)**

What Is a "Post-Evangelical"?
Several people have suggested to me that the term *post-evangelical* is really just a fashionable way of saying *ex-evangelical*. However, properly used, post means something quite different from ex. *Post*, which means *after*, has connotations of *following on from*, whereas ex implies ceasing to be. Taking this into account, *to be post-evangelical is to take as given many of the assumptions of evangelical faith, while at the same time moving beyond its perceived limitations*. Linguistically, the distinction is similar to the one that sociologists make between the modern and postmodern eras. In order for something to be postmodern it has to build on, or be linked with, or contiguous to, modernity.

My thesis is that post-evangelicals differ from evangelicals especially in that they are influenced by a different culture than the one that shaped present-day evangelicalism. Sociologists and philosophers believe that Western societies are undergoing a major cultural shift, away from what they call modernity to postmodernity—a shift we'll examine more closely in chapter six. For the time being, we should note that during most of the twentieth century, evangelicals experienced and express their faith, and contended for the integrity and credibility of their faith, in the cultural environment of modernity. Post-evangelicals, on the other hand, live in an increasingly postmodern cultural environment. Consequently postmodernity influences the way they think about and experience their faith. Postmodernity has become the new context in which the integrity and credibility of their faith must be tested.

Many people will feel uneasy about this close connection between faith and culture; some may even argue that their faith is based

a symbol of hope

on truth unaffected by culture. But nowadays, such a naïve view is impossible to sustain; nearly all scholars, evangelical or not, argue that our whole perception of the world—including our faith—is deeply influenced by culture and language. The way we perceive the being and person of God is influenced by culture, the way we think of redemption is influenced by culture, the way we imagine heaven is influenced by culture, and the way we approach the Bible is influenced by culture.**(j)**

> **(j)** Missionaries have always understood this. How can it be that the same denominations and societies that support global missions won't admit that much of what they think of as "Christianity" might actually be cultural?
> —**Holly Rankin Zaher**

The idea that we can simply pick up the Bible and read it, apart from any cultural conditioning is, quite frankly, nonsense. In fact, a great gulf lies between the cultural world of the Bible and our own world. We can (and do) seek to bridge that gulf, with the Spirit's illuminating help, through biblical scholarship, but the gulf is there all the same.

The implications of these cultural differences for spirituality and theology are enormous. It's probably fair to say that the post-evangelical impetus generally begins in individuals as a growing awareness of small but irritating differences between how they and their evangelical friends view things like worship style, church music, language, attitudes toward the rest of the world, or political assumptions. Before long, differences begin to appear with regard to spirituality and theology as well.

One of the hallmarks of post-modern culture is a longing for the spirituality squeezed out by modernity's emphasis on materialism and rationalism.**(k)**

> **(k)** In his book **Postmodernity**, David Lyon cites consumerism and new information technologies as the reasons for this cultural shift. Our consumeristic attitude toward religion is a natural outgrowth of capitalism. What if we stopped marketing Christianity? Would it be more authentic?
> —**Holly Rankin Zaher**

In his excellent book *What Is the New Age Saying to the Church?*[3] John Drane demonstrates that this spiritual hunger has largely been satiated by the New Age movement rather than by the church. The post-evangelical impetus, however, is to search for this fresh sense of spirituality, which they don't find in most evangelical circles, in the symbolic and contemplative traditions of the church rather than in the New Age movement. Celtic Christianity, as well as aspects of Catholicism and

the post-evangelical

Eastern Orthodoxy, is often helpful.**(l)** Not only do post-evangelicals want to feel a surge of fresh spirituality, but they also want to understand their faith, so they have a healthy appetite for theology. At the same time, the influence of their culture turns them away from the certainty and absoluteness of much evangelical theology. Post-evangelicals are more comfortable with the mysteries, ambiguities, and paradoxes of faith. So where do they turn? This is a key question, and one which we will tackle before we are through.**(m)**

The only other thing I need to say at this point regarding the nature of the term *post-evangelical* is that it certainly doesn't describe a movement, as such. Drane says that the nature of the New Age movement is that relatively few people actually label themselves "New Agers," although an enormous number of people identify with some aspects of what *New Age* stands for.[4] It's fairly similar with post-evangelicalism: a lot of people who've never even heard the term—much less used it as a self-conscious label—will, I believe, identify strongly with much of what we are discussing. And they may not all be evangelicals.

Footnote: And This Is Me

By way of a footnote to this introductory chapter, it may help if I say a few things about myself and the rather unusual church I was, until recently, deeply involved with, as I shall be making references to it throughout the rest of the book.

My background is thoroughly evangelical. I grew up in a Brethren Church and made a personal commitment of faith as a young teenager. Later, in another setting, I received what was called the baptism of the Holy Spirit. My Brethren Church subsequently asked me either to renounce this baptism of the Holy Spirit, or leave the church. They believed, with many others, that the baptism of the Spirit—which has subsequently become widespread throughout the charismatic movement—was unhealthy Pentecostal "emotionalism" and something definitely to be avoided. I did leave and became involved in the early house-church movement. When I reached the tender age of 22—now married to Pat and with a young family—we branched out and planted our first church. This was the start of 20 years of full-time work among house churches, a decade of which was spent leading a team of 15 people who gave oversight to some 50 churches.

Toward the end of the 1980s, Pat and I felt the need for a fresh focus in our lives. Without intending to do so, we became caught up with people who were either on the fringes of evangelical and charismatic churches or who had fallen off the edge altogether.**(n)**

(n) Last year, a seminary student told me, "I feel like I'm at the edge of the set in **The Truman Show**, and I'm asking, 'Is this all there is to evangelicalism? There has to be more.' I don't know what to do, but I thought that you might understand." Post-evangelicals must create the space where we can have these conversations, ask questions, muse, dream, laugh, and cry.
—**Holly Rankin Zaher**

Pat and I found ourselves rethinking theological issues and especially the way churches (from all traditions) tend to demand conformity over and above the essential requirements of the gospel. We were amazed to discover how many ex-churchgoers there were around, people who, though they no longer attended church, still believed. We also met some people at the Greenbelt Arts Festival, a U.K. styled music and arts gathering for both Christians and non-Christians, who treated the event as their "church," even though Greenbelt is a once-a-year engagement!

I'm now convinced that these people are just the tip of an enormous iceberg. Tens of thousands of people continue to practice their faith privately while finding no real relevance for church in their lives. I don't mean to imply that all of these people are post-evangelical as I'm describing it in these pages. However, if that option had been available to them in church, I'm certain that many of them would still be attending.

Believing that Christianity is, in essence, a communal faith, Pat and I and a few other friends began to experiment with a different form of church that might appeal to at least some of these people. The upshot was a rather unconventional church, facetiously called Holy Joe's, which meets in the lounge bar of a South London pub on Tuesday nights. In spite of its weaknesses, Holy Joe's demonstrates that alternative models for church life are possible. Holy Joe's has also become a symbol of hope for people in many parts of the country even when they never attended one of its meetings. I have often talked with people who have given up on church, but say, "If only there was something like this where I live." From time to time we also hear of other similar ventures, in Britain and in other countries, sometimes inspired by Holy Joe's, and sometimes not.

The format is simple and the atmosphere very relaxed. People behave as they normally would in any pub—they drink or smoke, they can participate as much or as little as they wish, and if they don't like it, they can move to the main bar. We have worship evenings, which tend to be quite contemplative, with plenty of candles, symbols, and ambient music; we have Bible study evenings during which attendees eagerly try to understand and interpret the Scriptures. Holy Joe's does not set itself up against the traditional churches—several ex-members are now training for ordination in the Church of England—but it is satisfying a need that many churches have failed to meet. I am not saying that this sort of thing is the only way ahead for post-evangelicals—the vast majority will probably (hopefully) remain in their churches. But Holy Joe's is an example of how one group of post-evangelicals is trying to work out their faith communally.(o)

(o) Once the excitement of being "a new kind of Christian" wears off, post-evangelical churches like Holy Joe's may find themselves stuck with the mundane and ordinary aspects of community life—meeting budgets, refurbishing the social hall, putting up with cranky old Mr. Wilson. The test of post-evangelicals' maturity will be how they live through that stage.
—Mark Galli

02

just when we
thought we had
all the answers..

just when we thought we had all the answers...

This chapter replaces my original second chapter, which gave an overview of developments in British evangelicalism over the last 30 years or so. Although it set the scene for this book, that chapter was relevant primarily to British readers. For this reason, I felt it necessary to ask an American to give an equivalent version for American readers. I am delighted with Joseph R. Myers' contribution. It effectively blends into the overall flow of the book while setting the North American context for post-evangelicalism.

—*Dave Tomlinson*

Revolution and Reformation

While American evangelicalism gained new power and visibility with the rise of megachurches during the 1980s, its roots are actually much older. In fact, the seeds of American evangelicalism already had been planted by the time of the Revolutionary War.**(a)**

(a) Most scholars argue that to understand the advent of American evangelicalism, you first have to understand the Great Awakening—including the theology and practice of George Whitefield, John Wesley, and Jonathan Edwards. The American revolution is a secondary consideration.
—**Mark Galli**

During this time, the British Parliament wielded power over the colonies arbitrarily, which exasperated the colonists. The Quebec Act of 1774—which gave Canadian Catholics the power to collect taxes and exercise other customary privileges usually reserved for European Catholics—was "one of the last straws that broke the back of the British-American relations."[1] This act inflamed the already smoldering colonists because the British government gave Quebec liberties the colonists were seeking but denied.

But the residents of the thirteen colonies perceived something else in the Quebec Act. To them, it represented the establishment of Roman Catholicism right on their doorsteps. And the Catholic faith represented the Inquisition, religious tyranny, and the end of religious freedom. Americans' worst fears were confirmed— Parliament cared so little for freedom that it would establish a religious despotism in the outposts of America. What could prevent tyranny moving south and east from Quebec to cover the entire New World?[2]

the post-evangelical

(b) Historians, by way of contrast, believe the American Revolution and Constitution both were shaped by a mixture of Christian and Deist sensibilities, which helps explain so many contradictions and paradoxes in American history—and in evangelicalism. To misunderstand this is to misunderstand the paradoxical nature of evangelicalism in American culture.
—**Mark Galli**

When the colonists won the Revolutionary War, evangelicalism—armed with the momentum and righteousness of victory—exploded onto the American frontier. Many evangelicals thought of *American* and *Christian* as being synonymous. Each shaped the worldview of the other.**(b)**

Ultimately, however, the worldview of America's evangelicals was rooted in the 95 theses nailed to the Wittenberg door.

> The Reformation was far more than a rising up of irate lay people against corrupt and exploitative priests, and it was much more than a mere theological row. It was a far-reaching social movement that sought to return to the original sources of Christianity. It challenged the idea that divine authority should be mediated through institutions or hierarchies, and it denied the value of tradition. Instead, it offered radical new notions of the supremacy of written texts (that is, the books of the Bible), interpreted by individual consciences. The Reformation made possible a religion that could be practiced privately, rather than mainly in a vast, institutionalized community.[3]

Upon this foundation, between 1776 and the 1960s, "America shifted from a nation in which most people took no part in organized religion to a nation in which nearly two thirds of American adults do."[4] Along the way, evangelicals led America in adopting these basic beliefs:

- freedom of religion
- salvation is found in Jesus alone
- the centrality and authority of Scripture

(c) Generally Americans don't collectively "believe" any one thing. Even when, during the antebellum era for instance, evangelicalism was culturally dominant, a significant number of Americans belonged to other traditions, from Roman Catholicism to Transcendentalism to skepticism.
—**Mark Galli**

- the privatization and individualistic practice of faith
- tradition has little value
- the gospel message is simple enough to be understood by all who read it.**(c)**

just when we thought we had all the answers...

The Tectonic '60s

During the 1960s and early 1970s, the Christian, and largely evangelical consensus in American culture was rocked by new cultural developments. President Kennedy was assassinated. The war in Vietnam escalated while support for the war dwindled at home. Hippies transformed college campuses into hotbeds of political dissent. Youth listened to Bob Dylan and John Lennon but tuned out their parents. They questioned all authority—and authority answered in mostly unsatisfactory and superficial ways. Many among this generation cried, "God *is* dead!" and "Clapton *is* God!"

Institutions also came under suspicion. The church did not escape the effects of this shifting ground. What had seemed certain one Sunday was under siege the next. Absolute truth was treated like absolute myth. To many the church became irrelevant.**(d)**

(d) Even so, during the 1960s and 1970s, conservative churches continued to grow. This is why Dean M. Kelly's **Why Conservative Churches Are Growing** (Harper and Row, 1972) created such a stir in its day. Recent history may have rocked evangelicalism, but most American evangelicals have generally remained happy with it.
—Mark Galli

However, the sixties generation did share their ancestors' dream of religious freedom. They wanted freedom from institutional faith. They wanted to be free to experience God personally. They wanted women to be free to serve as religious leaders. They wanted freedom for all ethnic groups to worship together. If freedom meant anything at all it meant freedom and participation for all.**(e)**

During the tectonic 1960s, everything seemed to change—music, family, education, sex, and, yes, even what it meant to be an evangelical Christian. The words evangelicals had historically relied upon didn't have much authority or power in this new culture. The divide between liberal and conservative Christians widened. Many evangelicals became more strident, dug in their heels and shouted

(e) Yes, the '60s launched a reaction to the church **institution**, but it wasn't a reaction to evangelicalism. A revolution with a name like "The Jesus Movement" is not exactly a battle cry against evangelicals. Mostly it was a repudiation of institutional rigidity, corporate bureaucracy, and the church's embrace of dominant cultural values: patriotism, consumerism, materialism, and the franchising of Christianity. The basic beliefs Joseph lists at the beginning of this chapter were eagerly embraced by the Jesus Movement as well. In fact, many went beyond evangelicalism to become "hippie fundamentalists." The Calvary Chapel movement that rose from the Jesus Movement is so committed to "sola scriptura" that sermons are restricted to biblical exposition. What happened in the '80s and '90s was the yuppyization of evangelicalism, which meant that evangelicals could once again embrace patriotism, consumerism, materialism, and the franchising of Christianity.
—Mike Yaconelli

louder. Most evangelicals bemoaned the way popular culture castigated preachers and clergy as court jesters for an old, sickly monarch.

The Return of the Evangelical, Better Than Ever
Over time, however, and especially from the early 1980s to the mid-1990s, American evangelicalism experienced a marked resurgence.

> Today, not only has decline in church attendance apparently bottomed out, but many evangelical churches are growing dramatically and new churches are being planted regularly. High-profile personalities in politics, entertainment, and sports are continually "coming out" about their faith, and the media pays increasing attention to evangelical and charismatic issues.[5]

Evangelicals cheered as the baby boomers' children arrived. Finally, they sighed, a generation that understands the values that built this great country! The bourgeoisie returned, and yuppies started to fill the pews. Capitalism was rehabilitated in the 1980s—spearheaded by the policies and attitudes of the Reagan administration. Solid evangelical morals gained cultural currency, and a renewed passion for family was evident. The evangelical seedlings planted prior to the 1960s (and left for dead in the brushfire of the 1960s) grew and thrived beyond expectations. But these seedlings were not exactly the same as those planted by earlier evangelicals. Some grafting had taken place.

The "Charismaticizing" of Mainstream Evangelicalism
I grew up a fundamental evangelical. It was a good place to grow up. I remember how sermons I heard in the early 1970s insisted that the foundational, fundamental beliefs of evangelicalism were beyond doubt and above reproach. Many sermons I heard also took strong issue with the charismatic movement. I can remember being sent to my room for suggesting that raising one's hands might not only be acceptable, but also biblical!

> Initially, during the late 1960s and early 1970s, the renewal movement threatened to split evangelicals irreparably; the terms "evangelical" and "charismatic" were almost totally incompatible.

just when we thought we had all the answers

To some degree this arose from the fact that many evangelicals reacted violently to renewal, in some cases denouncing it as of the devil. There was also the fact that the renewal cut across the old denominational barriers—even Protestant and Catholic—uniting people with a stronger bond than did identification with evangelicalism. The acrimony and pain created by the early divisions was enormous: even previously close friends and colleagues vilified one another in the name of truth.

By the end of the 1970s, however, much of the heat had gone from the issues; there was calmer dialogue between charismatic and non-charismatic evangelicals, and more acceptances of one another. Fifteen years later, the situation has changed dramatically: it is now clear that the whole center ground of evangelicalism has become gradually charismaticized, adopting the style and ethos of the charismatic movement.

Overall, charismatic renewal, which initially threatened the unity and well-being of evangelicalism, has actually proved to be a powerful source of its energizing. Of course the appeal is by no means universal: there are still many evangelicals who resist the tide of the charismatic. [6]

After a few decades of cultural ridicule, *powerful* and *energizing* were two words evangelicals were glad to welcome back into the vocabulary.

A New Generation of Evangelical Leaders Emerges
Church leaders in the 1960s grasped for ideas they thought would help turn the tide. They realized that a new way of doing church was required if they were to attract the youth culture. The youth ministry movement sprang from this search.

Youth pastors were hired to bring youth back into the church. They were given great latitude and granted a high tolerance for mistakes and disasters. Youth rooms, gymnasiums, and family-life centers adorned the church's landscape. Christian education programs listed "junior church," "rap sessions" (topic-oriented discussions), and culturally relevant classes on drugs, music, and sex.

As these youth matured and began assuming leading roles in congregations, they brought some of the secular youth movement's ideology with them. These new leaders were not formed by the "business blue" of old IBM; they spoke the new language of the "client service culture." They were more tolerant, experimental, and experiential. And, on the whole, they are:

- charismatically inclined, if not full-blown charismatics;
- still theologically fairly conservative;
- socially and politically and even environmentally aware;
- eager to promote evangelical values within society, as well as the evangelize individuals."[7]

Over time these leaders have met little resistance. While not "doing it like it had always been done," they were resuscitating evangelicalism.

Piggyback Success

As evangelicals recovered a sense of health, the old guard began to flex their reenergized muscles. Jim Bakker's PTL Club ruled the sacred screen; Jimmy Swaggart ran a close second. Billy Graham filled outdoor stadiums like a rock star. There were more television stations and programs dedicated to religious programming than ever before. Contemporary Christian music—with its evangelical message—crossed over to the mainstream.

Publisher's Weekly admitted that some religious books were actually outselling New York Times bestsellers. Large secular publishers took notice and entered the market by securing Christian authors and publishing companies. In some markets, newspaper religion pages blossomed into stand-alone sections.

Large, nondenominational events like Promise Keepers trumped denominational gatherings. These gatherings capitalized on the strength of large-group worship while also offering short, intense educational opportunities. Cutting-edge evangelical thinkers and practitioners were brought in as powerful speakers. Laity was powerfully equipped for ministry.

The recovery of evangelicalism was also marked by resurgent political muscle. The "Silent Majority" spoke loudly and voted. Polls checked the pulse of the evangelical heart. Billy Graham, Jesse Jackson, and Bill Hybels were presidential spiritual advisors. Pat Robertson was a viable presidential candidate for the religious right.

Even now, evangelicals carry a big, influential stick through the political landscape. On July 27, 2002 the *Washington Post* ran the following headline: "Evangelical Leaders Ask Bush to Adopt Balanced Mideast Policy." In the early summer of 2002, a court in California ruled that the U.S. pledge of allegiance was unconstitutional because it contained the phrase "under God." Evangelicals flooded the phones of talk shows and state representatives. By summer's end they had their way. "Against this very positive background, it is understandable that many would ask, 'Why on earth should we be discussing "post"-evangelicalism?' After all, we've never had it so good."[8] And yet, evangelicalism's resurgence isn't the whole story, either.

The Great American Pastime

When I was a boy, baseball was life—and life was baseball. My friends and I would gather in the park to play ball all day long. During the long winters, we played sockball in the garage. We marked lines on the walls—home run, triple, double, single, and an automatic out area—and tried to hit the tubesock.

At school casual discussion almost always came back to baseball. We'd argue in defense of our favorite big-league team; we'd extol the virtues of our own little league or neighborhood team.

We weren't the only ones concerned with these issues. We heard our fathers and grandfathers argue over the same teams and players. Family time was often spent watching the home team on the TV or at the park. We knew what everyone meant by "America's pastime." And we loved being part of it.

Major and minor league baseball has experienced significant growth since then. New stadiums are architectural marvels. Individual players today often receive more compensation in a year than a team full of players from my childhood days would make in a lifetime. There are more televised games and more spectators than ever before. Baseball has come a long way.

So why was there virtually no public outcry during the 2002 season when players threatened to strike? Why did so few people seem to care? After all, isn't baseball America's great pastime?

the post-evangelical

Well...what if baseball has also become the great American *pasttime*? In the world of sports, baseball barely makes the top five. Football, NASCAR (and motor sports in general), and basketball all rank higher when it comes to fan interest. And the troubled waters may run even deeper. Look at the American playground: Reality-based TV, the WWF, video games, and extreme sports are all gaining. The club in someone's hand today is usually a golf club, not a bat.

Could it be that, just at the pinnacle of baseball's "success," we've become culturally post-baseball?

Just When We Thought We Had All the Answers...
And, could it be that just at the pinnacle of evangelicalism's success, we've become culturally post-evangelical? Especially since the ultimate measure of evangelical success shouldn't be confused with the "bottom-line" power, influence, and growth measures commonly used by big business?

Just when evangelicals thought they had all the answers, someone changed all the questions. It's helpful here to remember that the evangelical movement was fueled by the modernist cultural worldview. The Enlightenment, the Age of Reason and rational thought, the scientific method, and the resulting Industrial Age were turbochargers for evangelical combustion. But now the culture is in the midst of a major shift in its worldview, a shift signaled by the tectonic sixties, but actually deeper and more pervasive—and the fuel for evangelicalism is running out at the moment of its greatest triumph.**(f)**

(f) The fuel for evangelicalism is not so much running out as the increasing longing for God is making fuel unnecessary. What used to matter to evangelicalism doesn't matter anymore—not because it isn't true, but because it's obsolete. Instead of worrying about prepositional truth, biblical authority, and absolute truth, they're still concerned about dancing.
—**Mike Yaconelli**

As a result, as evangelicals adapt to the new postmodern culture they find themselves in, they are beginning to shift on some of their traditional stances. The rest of this book explains how and why these shifts are taking place. At this point, however, it would be helpful to highlight some of the shifts:

• from propositional expressions of faith to relational stories about faith journeys.
• from the authority of Scripture alone to a harmony between the authority of Scripture and other personal ways God mysteriously

and graciously speaks to Christians.
• from a theology that prepares people for death and the afterlife to a theology for life.
• from a personal, individualistic, private faith to harmony between personal and community faith.
• from anti-Catholic and anti-nonprotestant perspectives to greater acceptance and curiousity about other approaches to knowing God.
• from the church being a place where people take up space to the church as a mission outpost that sends people out.
• from an approach to missions that emphasizes mass conversions by individuals to "share the good news with the whole world" approach.
• from arguing faith to the "dance of faith."[9]
• from salvation by event to a journey of salvation.
• from a salvation of humanity to a salvation of all creation.
• from a Western, American understanding of the gospel to a worldwide view.
• from motivating through fear to motivating through compassion, community, and hope.[10]
• from a search for dogmatic truth to a search for spiritual experience.

These changes will be examined in more depth in chapter six. For now, however, note that the rules of engagement have changed. Our culture is moving away from the ideologies that made evangelicalism so welcome and effective up to now. The promises of science and an evangelical approach to theology and truth modeled on science's success are being challenged by a new search for spirituality.

I believe we are only now feeling the enduring cultural aftershocks of the 1960s quake. Many are calling the transition "postmodern" and the evangelical response a "shift toward post-evangelical." Even as the heart of the gospel remains the same, Christianity continues to affect the culture and be affected by the culture. God is still at work. Who can define what the future expression of the church will be?
—Joseph R. Myers

worlds apart

worlds apart

As I've already stated, the post-evangelical impulse often draws its initial strength from the sense of irritation many people feel with evangelical "culture." If the irritation arose merely on account of differences of taste over music or film or style of dress, it could doubtless be fairly easily overcome. People are more tolerant about such things these days. Other issues, however, about matters most evangelicals think are essential to the Christian faith, also feed the post-evangelical impulse.

Whatever our background or tradition, we are all tempted to absolutize our own notion of what is essential to the Christian faith. Of course this is not simply a modern problem—members of the early church faced it, too. Probably the biggest threat to the first-century church came not from outside but from within, in the form of the rift over Judaism. Many Jewish Christians argued that new Gentile believers must submit to Jewish law in order to be real Christians. Paul would have none of it, so the issue had to be cleared up at the Council of Jerusalem (Acts 15:1-29). After much debate the synod sent a letter to the Gentile believers that stated, "It seemed good to the Holy Spirit and to us not to burden you with anything beyond the following requirements…" The particular religious and cultural issues under consideration then are of little consequence to us today, but the underlying struggle to contextualize the Christian faith in new cultural situations—to make sure that it is proclaimed and lived in both a culturally relevant and biblically coherent manner—is of crucial importance. I will now illustrate this with some concrete examples.**(a)**

Christian missions have repeatedly brought the issue of what is biblically non-negotiable, and what is culturally variable, to the fore. In the past foreign missionaries often sought more than a change of heart from the indigenous peoples to whom they proclaimed the gospel; they imposed a change of culture on them as well. Kwame Bediako, a Presbyterian theologian from Ghana, speaks painfully of the way missionaries wreaked havoc on

(a) The gospel of Jesus has always found its way in new cultural settings, and not only by changing its methods, but also making adjustments to the message. Those who hold to a biblical understanding of the gospel are keenly aware that the gospel Jesus proclaimed was Good News that began with the blessing of Abraham. The Good News is good in particular contexts. It is not the case, as some seem to wishfully say, that the gospel is always the same. Can you imagine Christianity if we were left only with an expression of the activity of God from a past culture and time?

Those seeking to be "post-evangelical" and not anti-evangelical will always seek to keep the best of evangelicalism. This should be the understanding that the gospel is living and active in our world and is as fitting to our setting as any point in history.
—**Doug Pagitt**

the post-evangelical

African culture in the name of the gospel. Their tendency, he says, was "to treat anything pre-Christian in Africa as either harmful, or at best value-less, and to consider the African once converted from paganism as a sort of *tabula rasa*, on which a wholly new religious psychology was some-how to be imprinted."[1] This cultural presumption, insists Bediako, amounted to a contemporary "judaizing" activity that failed to trust converts to the Holy Spirit's guidance. Quoting an African missiologist, Bediako says that the major weakness in the Western missionary movement in Africa lay in the fact that Africa had no Paul![2] **(b)**

> **(b)** Rereading Paul's letter to the Philippians, I'm intrigued and challenged by his confidence that the Holy Spirit will work in that community. He writes, "I hope all of you who are mature Christians will agree on these things. If you disagree on some point, I believe God will make it plain to you. But we must be sure to obey the truth we have learned already" (Philippians 3:15-16, NLT). Churches are God's domain, and not that of his disciples or apostles. Post-evangelicals are talking like Bediako, trying to identify how we've domesticated the gospel and how that gets in the way of proclaiming it.
> **—Timothy Keel**

Middle-class values form the dominant cultural norm in most evangelical churches, and these values function much like the Old Testament ceremonial laws did for the judaizers in the early church. These values, however, warp the very nature of the gospel. Of course, the term "middle class" is notoriously difficult to define. The old Marxist definition, based on purely economic factors, no longer meets the complexities of the contemporary situation. Today, most people use the term to describe an attitude that's conservative and committed to maintaining traditional ideas about society, family, and personal morality. Though this attitude represents a valid point of view, it is also problematic. First, a middle-class attitude generally fuels an upwardly mobile, materialistic, lifestyle that has ominous implications for church and society. In his challenging book *A Long Way from Home*, Tony Walter says that as Christians aspire to move up the social ladder they gradually surround themselves with the trappings of a suburban lifestyle. This climb usually involves moves to housing in better areas. Walter argues that the overall effect is to increase the resources of suburban churches at the expense of churches in poorer areas.[3]

But second, the more significant problem is that these middle-class evangelicals (and they are not alone in this) also create what Walter refers to as "culture religion." That is, they identify Christianity with the standards, values, and attitudes of their own limited and imperfect culture—in this case, middle-class culture:

Christians may not be aware of the extent to which they have conformed to a middle-class lifestyle. So many of the public values of society are middle class that these values, which are far from inevitable or God-given, are taken for granted. Some Christians, because they have one or two taboos—such as not drinking or swearing—that set them apart from other people, are able to convince themselves that they are not conforming to society. By focusing their attention on gambling or drink, they ignore the way in which they have unconsciously absorbed their neighbor's views on virtually everything else. They strain at a gnat and swallow a whole cultural mule.[4]

The consequence of confusing Christianity with middle-class values is that people who don't identify with that culture reject the church and, in many cases, the gospel, too.(c)

And this doesn't simply affect African or working class people; it also affects a whole stratum of people—especially younger people—who do not identify with the status quo of the establishment at all. One such person told me: "To be quite honest, there isn't much apart from faith in Jesus that I share in common with these people; but the frightening thing is that they seem to feel sure I will 'improve' and become like them, given a bit of time and some working on by the Holy Spirit. I doubt if I will stay around that long."(d)

There is no shortage of examples for how middle-class values and Christian standards are often muddled together. We will look at just two broad areas.

(c) For many post-evangelicals there is great interest in life with God as an alternative to the future promised by the American Dream. The expressions of the post-evangelical church around the world are often from younger people with hopes and dreams that extend beyond what their culture offers. This calls post-evangelical churches to adjust their message, the way they're structured, and the way money is used. In our community, our post-evangelical sensibilities have led us to attempt to live differently with our money and resources. In contrast to evangelical churches I have been involved with—that found great resonance with being a people of fine buildings and appointments in an effort to give the best we have for God—our community seeks to live thriftily in the world. Our post-evangelical sensitivity implores us to live beyond the American Dream that so strongly recruits the youth of America.
—**Doug Pagitt**

(d) We must stay quite aware that there is no "clean" version of Christianity. All expressions of Christianity are culturally affected, and that is a good thing. Therefore, we must resist any temptation to say that one understanding of Christianity is more pure or closer to that of Jesus'. Post-evangelicals are not expressing better Christianity, only a more fitting one for their setting.
—**Doug Pagitt**

the post-evangelical

The Normative Nature of the Traditional Nuclear Family

Evangelicals generally see the preservation of traditional family values as a key social cause. I have no doubt that post-evangelicals share some of their concerns. Few subjects, however, better illustrate the differences between traditional evangelicals and post-evangelicals than the family. The big question is, *What do we mean by family values?* For most evangelicals, family values are associated with a particular model of family—the modern "nuclear" family. Even though this family model bears little resemblance to the multigenerational, extended family that existed in biblical times it has a kind of sacred status for evangelicals.

From a middle-class evangelical perspective, "family values" means first and foremost the *sanctity of marriage*—that is, the lifelong commitment of one man and one woman within a legally recognized marriage.

Christians of all persuasions agree that lifelong, faithful partnerships are desirable. There may be less agreement, however, about whether such a partnership must be a state- and/or church-sanctioned marriage. The concept of living together without a marriage ceremony has become an accepted social norm. From the evangelical point of view, such arrangements are almost invariably unacceptable, since couples that simply live together are not counted as married and are consequently "living in sin" (though the phrase is somewhat out of vogue). Many post-evangelicals, however, are troubled by this simple equation, especially since, from their perspective, many of those cohabiting are Christians as deeply committed to their relationship as any formally married couple—perhaps even more so. In such situations, the desirability of a formal partnership is not what post-evangelicals are questioning. They do question the inflexibility of those unwilling to accept the validity of marriage when it exists in essence even though the traditional, culturally sanctioned marriage ceremonies were not observed.

Scripture nowhere insists on a specific ceremonial model for entering into marriage. In fact, some Scripture obscures as much as it reveals. Isaac's marriage to Rebekah, for example, is summed up with a terse description of Isaac bringing her to his mother's tent where, we are told, "He took Rebekah, and she became his wife." Talk about cutting out the formalities! Even the famous marriage at Cana that Jesus attended is silent about the "ceremony" that presumably took place, if not about the shortage of wine at the reception.

Most evangelicals believe the biblical notion of marriage incorporates at least three basic elements: a) the couple "leave and cleave"—that is, they move in together and live under the same roof, b) a covenant is created publicly between them, consisting in vows of faithfulness, and c) the relationship is consummated in sexual intercourse. According to this sort of definition cohabiting couples are only two-thirds married. "Ah yes," I hear people say, "but they are missing the most important ingredient." Perhaps. But might not an announcement to friends and family that they are committing to each other serve as a public covenant, even if the church and/or state isn't involved?

Now let me make my own position clear. By now Pat and I have been married for 35 years. We have not always experienced marital bliss. Pat has (very justifiably) been tempted to walk away on more than one occasion. She says the only thing that stopped her from doing so in the early years of our marriage was the realization that living with her mother was far less appealing than staying with me! But here we are, 35 years on, the very best of friends.

Would we still be together had we not made a public commitment all those years ago? I once posed this question to Pat in the midst of a lively session on the subject at Holy Joe's. Unnervingly, she paused before answering. Then she dropped the bombshell. "Well," she said pensively, "what everyone needs to know is that I haven't actually kept my wedding vows." Fifty pairs of eyes were glued to her as a stunned silence descended on the room. The only sound was the thumping of my heart. Even the jukebox in the bar downstairs seemed to scratch to a halt, and I could envisage all the clientele of the pub listening with cocked heads for the next line. "You see," she continued with perfect timing, "when we got married, I promised to *obey* ..." As the room resounded with laughter and applause, a sense of "phew" flooded my soul.

Ultimately I don't know what effect it would have had on our relationship had we not been formally married. I would like to think none at all. But I do know couples demonstrating the true spirit of marriage in relationships for two decades or more who were not formally wed.

My point is not to question the importance of marriage, but to plead for a significant distinction between a casual sexual or cohabiting relationship, and one in which two people are truly committed to each other. As Anne Borrowdale points out, "A cohabiting couple committed to an exclusive, permanent, faithful relationship [is] often said to be fulfilling the conditions of marriage, even though they have not gone through a ceremony."[5] And conversely, the presence of a wedding certificate in no way guarantees such a relationship. As Karl Barth once said, "Two people may be formally married and fail to live a life which can seriously be regarded as married life. And it may happen that two people are not married and yet, in their precarious way, live under the law of marriage." A wedding, he continues, "is only the regulative confirmation and legitimization of a marriage before and by society. It does not constitute marriage."[6] Adrian Thatcher makes a similar point: "The ceremony is the means of public recognition of a marriage relationship that already exists."[7]

> **(e)** Recent studies show that people who live together do not share the same level of trust and intimacy as married couples. The commitment entailed in marriage gives people more freedom to speak honestly without the fear that the other person is going to bolt.
> —**Mark Galli**

> **(f)** Downplaying the marriage "ceremony" or possession of a "wedding certificate" is dangerous because it relativizes "marriage." Of course a ceremony or certificate can be empty of meaning, but that doesn't mean we need to question marriage itself. An analogy: we don't disparage books because many are bad. Instead, we read, or try to write, good ones. We should insist on ceremonies and certificates that stand for something in marriage.
> —**Mark Galli**

It's true that couples that marry after cohabitation are more likely to divorce**(e)** although the reasons for this are by no means straightforward. Marriage is evolving in our society, and it is clear that whether people have or have not cohabited prior to a formal marriage does not guarantee a successful future for a relationship.**(f)**

I believe Christians still have an enormous amount of biblical wisdom to contribute in today's fluid situation—but we cannot contribute merely from a place of rigid traditionalism.

I am presently the vicar of an Anglican congregation with postmodern sensibilities. People appear at St Luke's at various stages in their relationships. I do not see it as my job to "police" these relationships, but to welcome them as travelers on a journey to and with Christ. Often couples decide that getting married is the next step for them, and no pastoral task pleases me more than conducting weddings. Let me tell you a story before moving on.

worlds apart

Janie and Simon share a lovely home, a mortgage, and two small children. I had no idea that they were not married when they appeared at church, so it came as a surprise when they recently asked me to marry them. Since they live several miles away, they wanted me to conduct the service in their local church for convenience's sake. I suggested they talk to the minister to seek his permission. To my astonishment he refused to allow the service in his church once he discovered that Simon had been previously married.**(g)** Eventually Janie and Simon decided to relocate the wedding to our church, where we had a glorious day celebrating the life the bride and groom already shared and gave thanks for their two super little boys.

> **(g)** While the idea of "policing" is unpopular, the church has always held people accountable to grow up in Christ. The church is not simply a collection of individuals on their own spiritual journeys, but a body that holds members accountable to mature in faith and life. Paul's teaching about sexual ethics is an early reflection of this concern that everyone grows toward more mature expressions of faith. One might grant new Christians some latitude, but eventually they also must be graciously held to biblical standards. To abdicate that responsibility and let "couples decide" can serve to reinforce the individualism so often deadly to church life.
> —**Mark Galli**

The story highlights the dilemma of middle-class Christianity-as-usual in a postmodern world. Gripping tenaciously to their precious "family values," churches frequently fail to see the forest for the trees in the complexity of human relationships. The mind boggles as to what "solution" Janie and Simon's local minister would have suggested to deal with the "problem" he perceived in their life. Actually I suspect he was more than happy to self-righteously wash his hands of the matter and leave it to someone else to sort out.**(h)**

> **(h)** It's striking that there's so little effort to understand why a minister would make this decision. While his decision seems extreme, charity requires that we give him the benefit of the doubt. Perhaps he had a very high view of marriage and believed that allowing divorced people to remarry would encourage a casual view of marriage.
> —**Mark Galli**

Another important element in the evangelical take on family values is that of proper *roles* and *responsibilities*. Evangelicals have traditionally believed family members should adopt specific roles. The husband is the head and, therefore, the final authority. As the main breadwinner, he is also responsible for providing for his family and for the behavior and discipline of the children. The wife's place is to support her husband and, if necessary, submit to him. As homemaker, she is responsible for domestic affairs and looking after the children. Together, both parents work to create a loving and disciplined atmosphere for their children.

Present-day evangelical attitudes are slowly changing. They recognize that many women need to, or choose, to work outside the home. This is deemed acceptable provided the children and home do not suffer. Marriage is now seen much more as a partnership where decision-making is a shared responsibility, even though the male "headship" is still affirmed.

Post-evangelicals, however, are heirs to a completely different, post-feminist culture. They assume sexual equality and take for granted the right of a woman to follow a career. They have no reservations about "house husbands," if that's what both partners agree upon, and they see no reason why men should be in charge. Family roles are negotiable.

There can be little doubt that evangelicals also see family as being a *two-parent* affair. There may be sympathy and support for single parents, but single parents are made to understand that they do not measure up to the ideal.**(i)**

(i) This has been a significant change for me since leaving a large, suburban, evangelical church and now pastoring a post-evangelical church in the center city of Minneapolis. The notion of the "God ordained" two-parent family simply becomes irrelevant to the situation in the city. I'm not advocating single-parent families at all, but I am suggesting that even two-parent families are insufficient in many settings in our world. Rather we need transformative communities in which families participate. This may be one of the reasons why evangelicalism is stronger in the suburbs than in urban settings. Suburbanites can more easily stay convinced that it's their "proper way of life with God" that makes things "work"; but in actuality it may be the solid cultural setting that keeps their faith in working order.
—Doug Pagitt

As a result, I know several single mothers who have left churches, tired of being patronized or of being made to feel that theirs are second-class families. Some have even been offered substitute fatherly input for the children. "They always seem to assume that I can't do as good a job," one angry mom said, "and yet I think I'm doing better than most of them."

Finally, we should mention the most basic assumption of all—that getting married or having a partner and eventually having children is the ultimate family-values norm. Singles are often asked, "When are you going to get married?" or "When are you going to have children?" An extremely blatant example of this attitude was experienced by a woman in her mid-30s with a reputation for being a "women's libber." When she told a group of (male) church leaders that she had no plans to get married, she was actually asked if she was a lesbian! When she replied (rather graciously, I think) that she was not, they said, "Oh, so you *will* get married if the Lord gives you a husband then?" Although this is an extreme instance of such prejudice, the underlying middle-class cultural assumptions made by these leaders (in spite of what Paul has to say about the spiritual benefits of being single!) are far from exceptional.**(j)** Such prejudices derive not from Scripture, but from the deeply embedded, middle-class cultural values.

> **(j)** Getting married and having children is the norm, biblically, historically, and sociologically. The problem isn't with the norm, but that Protestant churches don't have a good theology or system for honoring the celibate life—something that has always been the exception but should nonetheless be honored. Here evangelicals have something to learn from Roman Catholicism and Eastern Orthodoxy.
> **—Mark Galli**

Is there common ground on family values between evangelicals and post-evangelicals? Absolutely. Both agree on the importance of *love, commitment, faithfulness,* and *responsibility* as fundamental biblical principles and requirements. Families and family life are of crucial importance to us all, but as Tony Walter says, the healthy future of the family will be best ensured by putting it under scrutiny and by providing a critique of it rather than by absolutizing or idolizing it.[8]**(k,l)**

> **(k)** The early church was immersed in a pagan culture that accepted widespread homosexuality, cultic prostitution, philandering, and so on. In this situation the church felt no compulsion to change its ethics in order to gain a hearing from pagans. In fact, by holding rigidly its standards, the early church earned pagan respect, and eventually influenced the larger society to shore up its sexual ethics.
> **—Mark Galli**

> **(l)** There certainly is hope for common ground, but we should be aware that this might not mean common worship space or common leadership. The issues surrounding post-evangelical ministry expression are not simply about how and what people think, but are importantly played out in the expression of feelings and faith.
> **—Doug Pagitt**

The Confusion of Holiness with Respectability

"Joining the church is like joining a very exclusive club." I well remember the discomfort this statement brought me. It came from a man who had experienced a dramatic conversion to Christ from a life of heavy drinking, wife beating, and petty crime. He was entirely uncultured so far as Christian behavior was concerned, but the middle-class folk in the church I pastored were delighted to have such a "good catch." And for a while, they put up with his "inconsistencies" and lapses into old behavior.

But after a couple of months they decided he needed a "deeper work of God." They liked the fact that he had such a nasty past, but only for as long as he was becoming more like them. And so he felt as if the church was a club where he could never be a full member.

The matter came to a head one evening when three respected church members confronted me, and insisted I should put pressure on him to fit in and "let the Lord have full control of his life." I refused, saying that perhaps it was we who needed to listen to him. Then followed the ultimatum: "Either he goes, or we go." God knows, I needed their money, but I've never been very good with ultimatums. They left, and he stayed! Though he certainly continued to grow in his faith, he never did fit into the mold of the respectable Christian.

(m) We must also examine how the consumptive and materialistic nature of our culture has penetrated the church and evangelical ideas about lifestyle, marriage, and family. Individualism and mobility have destabilized not only families but also the institutions that once walked in step with families. The church bears much responsibility for taking on the wrong issues in public while privately ignoring (or even exalting) cultural values that are decimating community. We have strained out the proverbial gnat while swallowing a camel.
—Timothy Keel

This man was far from alone in feeling that the church is a kind of exclusive, middle-class club. Many people struggle with the church's expectation that they should change their behavior to fit in. Naturally, all groups, Christian or otherwise, have accepted behavioral norms and taboos. The problem with churches is that they so often equate their group's particular norms with behavior required of all Christians.(m) As we saw at the beginning of the chapter, this is not a new problem in the church. Taboos have existed since its inception. In more recent times, people like Dwight L. Moody condemned the perceived sins of the nineteenth century. What he described as "the four great temptations that threaten us today" were the theater, disregard for the Sabbath, Sunday newspapers, and atheistic teachings, including evolution.[9] All of these were still taboos in my early childhood in the Plymouth Brethren, along with going to the cinema, smoking, drinking, gambling, and even attending sporting events. And while the taboos in different churches differ from denomination to place, every church has them.

Nowadays, the ground has moved. Most of the temptations Moody inveighed against have become legitimate, while others, depending on the church community, remain off-limits. If in doubt, study the following:

A HELPFUL, UP-TO-DATE GUIDE TO CHRISTIAN BEHAVIOR

Smoking	No—not really	Some do in private (especially cigars).
Drinking	Okay	Not usually in bars, except nice ones.
Theatre/Cinema	Okay—yes	Provided it's wholesome.
Gambling	No	The Stock Exchange is acceptable.
Sunday Papers	Okay	Especially the *New York Times*.
Horoscopes	No	Some *do* have a sneaky look.
Premarital Sex	No	Never admit to it in public anyway.
Swearing	No—not really	Definitely not in public.

Facetious? Yes, but no less accurate for many church subcultures for being so.

Eat, Drink, and Be Compassionate

Those who visit Holy Joe's from other churches often give the impression of being ill at ease in a pub environment. As they look around at the apparent incongruity of people sitting in a pub, perhaps smoking, probably drinking, and yet talking, at times passionately, about God, Christianity, and the world in general, they invariably ask me what the difference is between Holy Joe's and the rest of the world. The question reminds me of a criticism Pharisees had of Jesus. "There is a glutton and a drunkard, a friend of tax collectors and sinners" (Luke 7:34). A better question is, In what ways are we supposed to be different from the rest of the world? And again, the wise answer of the apostles commends itself to us. Believers should not be saddled with greater burdens than is absolutely necessary. Rather than perpetuating religious taboos based on middleclass "family" values, Christians need to commit to that which is absolutely necessary and then leave the rest for people to decide for themselves. Tony Campolo reminds us of what is absolutely necessary:

> Both U.S. and U.K. evangelicalism have defined a Christian as someone more pious than the rest of the world. Personally, piety turns me off! The Christian is radically compassionate, not pious. What did people say about Jesus? They didn't call him pious! He had a lousy testimony. Did anybody ever call him spiritual? They

the post-evangelical

called him winebibber, glutton, someone who hangs around with whores and publicans. Jesus was too busy expressing compassion to measure up to the expectations of piety. And I think we need to be more Christlike.[10]

Without a doubt, many evangelicals are attracted to black and white, prepackaged, Christian morality. But there are many others who are tired of being *told* what is right and what is wrong. Their desire is to grow up in their faith, and they believe the only way to do it is by taking full responsibility for their thoughts, decisions, and actions. Sadly they often find that the evangelical environment isn't conducive to such growth. And we need to ask why.(n)

(n) We need reminding that being post-evangelical doesn't equal being grown-up. While there are certainly characteristics of a post-evangelical worldview that allow for a more mature faith in some areas, it's not in all areas and is in no way a given. Post-evangelicals will need to do the work that the evangelicals did in defining and calling people to maturity, and hopefully that maturity will be of greater and more useful value.
—Doug Pagitt

04

longing to grow

longing to grow

I want to tell you a couple of stories. The first is about Barbara, an MK (missionary kid). Although she grew up going to church with her folks, she had also been taught from quite an early age that she would need to come to a faith of her own. After going through university, where she developed her independence and thought about life for herself, she decided to make an open profession of faith in Christ at an evangelistic meeting she attended. Delighted and exhilarated, she went to a local evangelical church. Within three months her misgivings began to crystallize: "They just seemed so content with a faith that asked no questions," she told me. "Everyone calmly accepted whatever the leaders said."

She moved on and tried several similar churches, but always experienced the same disillusionment. "They appeared threatened by the level of my questioning," she continued, "and told me that I needed to let my doubts go and trust the Lord." Eventually Barbara faced the choice either to lay aside her questions and stick with this kind of church, or go elsewhere with her questions. She chose the latter, eventually joining a liberal Anglo-Catholic church. Thriving in her faith—questions and all—she says she will always be grateful for what evangelicals gave her but regrets that they could not take her any further.

The next story has not ended as well—yet! James was the minister of a thriving charismatic church. After years of burying his intellectual problems about Christianity under a sea of pastoral work and Sunday sermons, he suddenly hit a major inner crisis that he couldn't shrug off. I spent several hours walking round the local park listening to his endless stream of doubts and confusion. I told him I shared many of his questions and assured him that the pressure would diminish if he would be more open about his questions rather than bury them under a veneer of professionalism. Unfortunately he felt his situation wasn't that simple. "When I hinted to my deacons what I was feeling, they practically had kittens," he said. "They told me I was employed to build people's faith up, not to undermine it." Sadly, he has since left the church altogether and makes no profession of faith—but who knows?

These two post-evangelical accounts are typical. People flock to evangelical churches after profoundly helpful evangelical encounters, only to become disillusioned further down the road. Why does this happen to some people while other evangelicals apparently remain per-

the post-evangelical

fectly happy? In this chapter, we shall explore the question with the help of two psychological models.

Stages of Personal Growth(a)

It's now well understood that people pass through different stages in their personal development, and these stages have been analyzed in differed ways.[1] I've chosen a fairly straightforward, common sense example, M. Scott Peck's four stages of spiritual growth, which he discusses in his book, *The Different Drum.*[2]

In his psychotherapy practice, Peck noticed that religious people who came to him for therapy often finished the process as atheists, agnostics, or skeptics. On the other hand, atheists, agnostics, and skeptics often left therapy as deeply religious people. After puzzling over this for some time, he concluded the different reactions were connected to patients being in different stages of personal development. Like any model Peck's is an over-simplification, and most people fit somewhere on a continuum between the stages. I have changed some of Peck's wording, slightly, because it is ambiguous:

STAGE I:	Self-obsessed
STAGE II:	Conformist
STAGE III:	Individualist
STAGE IV:	Integrated

Stage I is characteristic of children, though Peck thinks about twenty percent of adults are also at this stage.(b)

The shift from Stage I to Stage II, usually as an adult, is often sudden and dramatic. Religious conversion can cause the shift, but so might some other important change of life, such as getting married, or even joining Alcoholics Anonymous.

longing to grow

Many dramatic conversions to Christianity take place in people who need a shift from Stage I to Stage II. Persons already in Stage II when they convert to Christianity will probably have less dramatic conversion experiences. Such converts might also feel inferior by interpreting the drama of another person's experience as a sign of greater divine power at work in them.

Peck maintains most believers and churchgoers are in Stage II. He calls this the "formal" stage because people in this stage are more attached to the form of religion than its essence. They vigorously oppose attempts to change canons, liturgies, or traditions. Stage II people prefer to see God as transcendent and struggle to accept God's immanence. They usually say that God is love, but their strongest image of God is one of judgment. Peck says, "It is no accident that their vision of God is that of a giant benevolent Cop in the Sky, because that is precisely the kind of God they need— just as they need a legalistic religion for their governance."

Despite the fact that Stage III people are frequently nonbelievers, "they are generally more spiritually developed than many content to remain in Stage II." Stage III—which Peck calls the skeptic stage—is full of doubt and questions. Some Stage III people sink into constant cynicism, which creates havoc for Stage II friends who cannot easily relate to doubt. As Stage III wears on, the doubt and cynicism usually fades and affirmations of faith begin to reappear, though not with the naivety of previous stages.

I call Stage IV "integrated." Not marked by the simplistic certainty of Stage II, people in Stage IV have an intuitive sense of wholeness or interconnectedness. Peck calls this the mystic-communal stage, because the drive for objective understanding has moderated under the sense of what cannot be fully grasped and yet is still to be sought after.

There are several important points about this matrix:

- The stages are *only milestones*. Multiple gradations exist within and between them.
- We all regress through earlier stages of our development in certain situations.
- The model is not pejorative. It *describes* stages we all pass through, but makes no claims about the rightness or wrongness of a particular stage.

the post-evangelical

• People can become Christians during any stage, and this will inevitably bear on the kind of conversion they experience, and their perspective on Christian life and faith in general.

(c) This may have less to do with "maturity" than with the nature of the movement. Like the military, evangelicalism is mission-driven. That's why evangelicals tend to appreciate authority, hierarchy, and clear explanations. These qualities help the movement fulfill its mission—winning a great many people to Christ. To disparage this is to misunderstand an essential aspect of evangelicalism.
—**Mark Galli**

Peck comments that Stage IV men and women will frequently enter religion through an attraction to mystery, whereas Stage II people enter religion to find concrete answers.**(c)**

I think, in a very approximate way, a lot of post-evangelicals are people who are moving from Stage II to Stage III. Their postmodern cultural experience is what usually jars them into this move. This does not make them any more intelligent or clever than those who remain content with Stage II, and their next steps can vary, as the two opening stories show. Incidentally, some post-evangelicals actually regress to Stage I and, not to put too fine a point on it, might be better described as pre-evangelical.

Why do so many folk who move to Stage III or IV feel a need to move on from evangelicalism to some other expression of the church, or to abandon formal churchgoing altogether? I think because the sociological (to say nothing of the theological and spiritual) environment of evangelicalism does not accommodate people at these stages as effectively and easily as it does those at Stage II. Perhaps this is because evangelical theology and morality are so definite. An environment that can comfortably accommodate Stage III people will be much freer with definitions and expectations, which all smacks of liberalism to the average evangelical.

Although Peck doesn't explore this possibility, it also seems to me that people who are otherwise in Stage II or III or IV tend to be at a lower stage when it comes to their religious lives. Peck's model—which concentrates on a straightforward progression through the stages—is not geared to deal with this phenomenon. So we shall now turn to a different model that explains how people sometimes switch patterns of behavior depending on the situation they find themselves in.

longing to grow

Child's Play

Transactional analysis, originated by Eric Berne and set out in his book *Games People Play*,[3] is based on the recognition that humans possess multiple natures. In the course of life, certain people or situations will activate one pattern of behavior, while other situations or people may evoke something quite different. Transactional analysis suggests three basic modes of behavior: Parent, Adult, and Child.**(d)** These terms are not to be taken literally; rather they refer to different kinds of emotional responses. Used in this technical sense the words are capitalized, to avoid confusion with more common usages.

> **(d)** Dave has some valid insights about the behavior of evangelicals, and it's interesting to compare them to Harris' Parent/Adult/Child model. Dave's observations may also be accurate, but the very people to whom he's writing this book are repelled by labels as much as the Child mode responses he describes.
> —**Mike Yaconelli**

Regardless of our age, most of us know what it's like to have a compliant Child reaction when we meet authority figures such as policemen, teachers, or even parents. It can suddenly and irrationally emerge, even though we know that such a response is no longer necessary. The Parent mode of behavior expresses itself through superiority. It majors in criticism, "shoulds" and "oughts," and verbal put-downs. The Adult pattern of behavior emerges when we feel accepted on equal terms, or when we feel respected and listened to. Each of these behavior patterns is triggered, says Berne, by mental and emotional recordings of earlier experiences we play back to ourselves subconsciously.

In his book *I'm OK—You're OK*, Thomas Harris demonstrates how people shift behavior patterns using the example of a 34-year-old woman who came to him with a problem of sleeplessness and worry about "what I am doing to my children." During the first part of a one-hour session, she wept and said, "You make me feel like I'm a three-year-old." When asked why she felt this way, she said, "I don't know. I suddenly felt like a failure." At a later point, when talking about her children, her manner and voice changed dramatically. She became critical and dogmatic: "After all, parents have rights, too. Children need to be shown their place." During this one-hour session the woman displayed three distinct personalities: one of the reasoning, logical, grown-up woman who entered therapy; one of the small child dominated by feelings; and one of a self-righteous parent.[4]

the post-evangelical

Many evangelicals relate to God and their Christian faith in the compliant Child mode. What is even more remarkable is the number of such people who have extremely well-developed Adult modes of behavior in other areas of their lives. A friend recently spoke with despair of the way in which doctors, lawyers, and business people in his church settled for an incredibly simplistic version of faith, despite their training and professional responsibilities. They walked into church, seemed to switch off their critical faculties, and proceeded to go along with virtually everything.

This problem is not limited to the intellectual dimension of faith. A disturbing number of evangelicals seem neurotic and suffer from a poor self-image. People—sometimes even pastors—explain the most mundane details of their lives in terms of God or the Devil. When something good happens, it's the Lord. "He helped me find this job," they say, or "God showed me what I should do." Bad things, on the other hand, are either the Devil's fault or traced back to a personal spiritual fault. Thus, "The enemy was really attacking me," or perhaps, "I should have been obedient to the Spirit." **(e)**

> **(e)** For many Christians, this language is the best they have to describe the spiritual dimensions of their lives. Many post-evangelicals might find it difficult to speak confidently about what God is doing in their lives, but that doesn't mean they have to disparage those who can. Granted, evangelical language is sometimes shopworn and robotic, but if we honor the spiritual experiences of skeptical post-evangelicals, we should also respect the more tangible religious experience of many evangelicals.
> —**Mark Galli**

All of these reactions are classic Child mode responses to a paternal Parent voice whispering in the background: "You mustn't question what God says," or "If you believe that, you'll go off the tracks," or "You must be obedient to God's word," or "If you obey God, everything will work out right."

Parental Pressure

Some people drop out of evangelical churches because of their dislike for a parental voice insisting that church membership hinges on accepting prescribed doctrines or codes of behavior. Sometimes the pressure to conform may be subtler—a look, a dropped invitation, implied criticism—yet no less powerful for that. Numerous evangelical churches and organizations will not allow speakers on their platforms unless they openly subscribe to an evangelical statement of faith. This Parental attitude fails to acknowledge that people who arrive at very different conclusions may nonetheless have done their theology with great integrity.

Fear of liberalism's "slippery slopes" isn't the only way the evangelical Parental voice speaks. The "shoulds" and "oughts" of the Parent are especially rampant in the area of Christian behavior. Evangelicals leave no doubt as to what is expected in their circles. Evangelical culture is laden with taboos, many of which owe more to middle-class respectability than longing for real holiness. These taboos often pressure people into living dual lives.

The dominant style of leadership in evangelical churches is also Parental. In the name of no-nonsense, no compromising, "give it to 'em straight" preaching of righteousness, we have a classic enactment of the paternal Parent, with inevitable responses of compliance or rebellion. "That's right," I hear someone say, "bring them to the point of decision." But is it the right decision?

The only decision that really counts is that which arises from genuine conviction, not coercion or the pressure of group dynamics. The apostle Paul speaks of sin reviving when the law comes, and he goes on to show that the law was powerless to affect real change (Romans 7 and 8).

A lot could be learned from modern management and teaching techniques in which old-style directional leadership has given way to an emphasis on facilitating people learning for themselves, making fully independent decisions—a much more Adult and, I believe, spiritual approach.

The Awakening Adult

As post-evangelicals endeavor to move beyond the compliant Child mode, they must take care that they don't simply switch to a rebellious Child mode, which is the flipside of compliance. Both compliance and rebellion are basically defenses against the imposition of authority, and they are equally ineffective means for making long-term progress. Paul's comments in Romans 7 indicate that rebellion is actually as much a manifestation of being under the law as the vain attempt to comply with its demands. What he speaks of in Romans 8 as being "in Christ" is a position

the post-evangelical

of faith that supersedes both rebellion and compliance.**(f)**

Transactional analysts also speak of a Child mode called "The Little Professor," or the awakening adult—a very helpful concept for our present reflections since it offers a constructive way forward. The Little Professor state is characterized by experimentation, inquisitiveness, creativity, and constant questioning. Post-evangelicals long to explore their faith without being shown the door. A young man who had grown up in an evangelical family spoke of the enormous relief he'd found in attending a post-evangelical group where he was able to openly explore questions he said would have "completely freaked" his parents. "I suddenly realized I could go wherever I wanted," he said. "It's a feeling that's both exhilarating and scary."

St. Paul's comments about being renewed in the mind are helpful here. All too often Paul's words are considered from a purely negative perspective, with the emphasis on what we *should not be thinking*. This is

typical of evangelicalism's Parental voice, which often defines what we're supposed to be by what we are *not* supposed to be. Of course we can interpret the renewed mind as one that's *not* paralyzed by greed, lust, and selfishness. But I think the term also suggests freedom to imagine how one might share, love, and encourage.**(g)**

longing to grow

The renewed mind has at least three qualities. First, it is an *open* mind willing to reconsider past positions. An *open* mind isn't gullible, but it thrives on doubts and questions, even when not governed by them. Open-minded people listen even the most outlandish ideas in the hope of learning something.

Second, the renewed mind is sensitive to *creative lateral* possibilities. Edward de Bono argues that much thinking is locked into straight furrows and mental ruts. Lateral thinking breaks out of these ruts to consider unusual and obscure connections between different ideas. The potential for this sort of thinking is unleashed by interdisciplinary studies and religious ecumenism. I no longer worry when people tell me, in Parent mode, "you can't do that" or "you'll end up watering it down." Evangelicals have made a god out of doctrinal and religious conformity. Humility suggests we should learn from others.

Third, renewed minds are reflective thinkers rather than merely repositories for new information. Harry Blamires writes: "The thinker challenges current prejudices. He disturbs the complacent. He obstructs the busy pragmatists. He questions the very foundations of all around him, and in so doing throws doubts upon aims, motives, and purposes which those running affairs have neither time nor patience to investigate. The thinker is a nuisance."[5](h)

One final element we should expect of the renewed mind is that it be *holistic*. Renewed minds make emotion, intuition, and mystery equal partners of rationality. Critical reason alone produces a false consciousness that's inevitably reductionistic. As we shall see, this is an important area of divergence between post-evangelicals and liberals, whose reliance on reason discounts cognitive contributions from the non-rational.

(h) Here Dave tackles one of the chief criticisms I often hear about postmodern culture. Many evangelicals believe postmodernism is just experiential and not intellectually reflective. Post-evangelicals will have to demonstrate that they don't treat the accumulation of experience the way modern evangelicals accumulated **knowledge**—and that they can be reflective and critical about both.
—**Holly Rankin Zaher**

liberals
in sheep's
clothing?

liberals in sheep's clothing?

And so to the crunch question: *Isn't post-evangelical just another way of saying "liberal in sheep's clothing"*? Among evangelicals, "liberal" is a code-word for anything that deviates from the evangelical line. My contention, however, is that while post-evangelical does mean something different than *evangelical*, it does not mean *liberal*. I would deeply regret a post-evangelical drift toward liberalism.

"The Boogie Man Will Get You!"

"If you go there, the boogie man will get you!" We've all heard parents use this ploy that trades on fear. Sometimes evangelicals will even use it to frighten Christians into conformity by raising the spectre of liberalism.

For example, I once heard a leading evangelical warn a well-known speaker, "If you carry on talking like that people are going to think you've gone liberal, and then doors are going to close and then..."

"I don't really care!" the speaker replied, boldly, thereby assuring no repeat invitation to that particular event.**(a)**

We shouldn't use pejorative and ultimately meaningless labels like "liberal" to make childish boogieman-type threats against each other. Our tentative and imperfect

> **(a)** I wonder what would've happened if the "leading evangelical" had lived in Jesus' day. I hope he would have said the exact same sentence to Jesus. ("People are going to think you've gone liberal, and before long, you'll find that you won't be seen as fully evangelical, and then doors are going to close.") Actually the doors did close for Jesus, and he ended up on a cross as a result. Closed doors and crosses have always been the result of following Jesus.
> —**Mike Yaconelli**

doctrinal deliverances matter little to God, and labels less. A sincere search for truth, on the other hand, does matter a great deal to God! Let me tell you a story about "The Evangelical Speaker and the Liberal Bishop."

Jesus told a parable to a gathering of evangelical leaders. "An evangelical speaker and a liberal bishop each sat down to read the Bible. The evangelical speaker thanked God for the precious gift of the Holy Scriptures and pledged himself once again to proclaim them faithfully. 'Thank you, God,' he prayed, 'that I am not like this poor bishop who doesn't believe your Word and seems unable to make his mind up whether or not Christ rose from the dead.' The bishop looked puzzled as he flicked through the pages of the Bible and said, 'Virgin birth, water into wine, physical resurrection. These things are hard to believe in, Lord. In fact, I'm not even sure I'm in touch with you in a personal way. But I'm

the post-evangelical

(b) Sorry, Dave, but this was not the wisest choice for a parable. The example of a bishop who says the virgin birth, et cetera, are hard to believe in, when connected to "this man was justified before God," is exactly the kind of statement critics will pounce on. Dave is defending openness by using an extreme example. Very few post-evangelicals I know are paralyzed by questions. The opposite is true. They have doubts about God and about Jesus, but the source of their doubts is the narrow evangelical definition of God and Jesus. Most post-evangelicals are evangelicals, but they can't fit their faith into the narrow, rigid mold evangelicals have constructed. They believe God is a mystery, which means he can't be contained or captured. They also believe God is a God of questions as well as answers, and post-evangelicals I know see questions as important as the answers. They believe in guarding the questions as well as the answers. This isn't belief in a vacuum, but belief that's alive, adventurous, and mysterious. This is belief that's passionate about what it knows and equally honest about what it doesn't. These post-evangelicals believe that not knowing is as important to faith as knowing.
—**Mike Yaconelli**

going to keep on searching.' I tell you" said Jesus, "that this liberal bishop, rather than the other man, went home justified before God. For those who think they have arrived have barely started out, but those who continue searching are closer to the destination than they realize."**(b)**

This version of the parable of the Pharisee and the tax collector attempts to highlight the original point Jesus made, but which we easily miss. We stand at the end of a long Christian tradition in which pharisaism is seen as synonymous with self-righteousness and hypocrisy. Jesus' original audience wouldn't have seen it this way. They thought Pharisees were men of great religious dedication and sincerity—the opinion most evangelicals today have about their own leaders. The original intent of the parable, however, was to overturn such values and prejudices.[1] What's more, the parable cuts both ways: my retelling of the parable for a gathering of liberal churchgoers would be the other way around!

(c) How do creedal affirmations function for post-evangelicals? Some hold that creeds should be public reminders of important confessional milestones for the Christian community. Others simply dismiss them as limiting and unhelpful tools for responding to God's work in their lives. I wonder whether ancient creeds birthed in response to ancient heresies call us to craft contemporary creeds in response to today's heresies?
—**Holly Rankin Zaher**

Ultimately, our church pedigrees, spiritual experiences, or creedal affirmations do not impress God.**(c)** St. Peter will not be asking us at the pearly gates which church we belonged to or if we believed in the virgin birth. The word *evangelical* will not even enter the conversation. A brief overview of how the present situation came about will help us understand why.

liberals in sheep's clothing?

The Parting of the Ways

During the seventeenth century, a major intellectual shift, known as the Enlightenment, ushered in the new intellectual and cultural reality now known as modernism. Before this change, medieval culture had been trapped by feudalism, ignorance, and superstition. Medieval religion was simplistic and authoritarian: God was the big boss in the sky, and his human subjects did his bidding without asking any questions. The church, earthly seat of God's authority, determined the meaning of truth, not only in the realm of religion, but in every other field as well: politics, science, history, art, and so on. To dissent was to be branded a heretic and risk persecution, excommunication, or worse.

Eventually, things began to change. René Descartes (1596-1650), one of the fathers of modern thought, sat down one chilly night, huddled up to the fire, and decided to question everything in his world—including his own existence. His momentous conclusion was that doubting his own existence was the only plausible demonstration that he really did, in fact, exist. Hence his famous dictum: *cogito ergo sum* ("I think therefore I am"[2]). Modest as this declaration sounds, it shifted the whole basis of epistemology—the study of how we know things—from old certainties dictated by the church to a new process of independent reason and doubt.**(d)**

(d) Epistemology is key. For modernists—whether conservative, evangelical, or liberal—faith is usually reduced to the cold, hard facts. For post-evangelicals, faith is integrated into all of life. Thus, in my context, I often hear conversations about social justice, the environment, simplicity, innovation, and the arts as we discuss faith.
—**Holly Rankin Zaher**

What Descartes essentially did was step out of his skin so that he could look upon himself as an object. And rather than viewing the world in a subjective way, as something he was inextricably connected to, Descartes and his successors suggested that the world could be viewed in an objective, detached fashion. As a consequence, the modern scientific method, which places a high value on dispassionate, objective examination, was developed. The benefits of the scientific method have been fairly obvious, although, as we shall see, there have been grave consequences too.

At this point, a brief introduction to some key terms related to Western culture's development will be helpful:

the post-evangelical

- The seventeenth- and eighteenth-century *Enlightenment* gave birth to what's known as *modernity*, the modern cultural outlook. *Modernity* looks at the world in a *critical* way that takes nothing for granted. This approach is closely identified with the scientific method, which attempts to examine the world objectively, that is, free from preconditions or dogma.
- The term *premodern* refers to the outlook that prevailed before the Enlightenment; it's sometimes also called *precritical*, since the prevailing religious, mythological, and superstitious attitudes of the day went virtually unchallenged.
- *Postmodernity* is a movement that's developed over the last few decades (although its roots go back much further) as a reaction to the exalted position modernity has given to reason and objectivity.

We could alternately express this as:

Premodern	Modern	Postmodern
Precritical	Critical	Postcritical
Superstition	Reason	Intuition
Mythology	Demythologizing	Remythologizing(e)

(e) At the 2003 Emergent convention, Chris Seay suggested that the Reformation may well have unnecessarily annihilated certain prevailing ideas and practices. He wondered whether or not we might be doing the same during the current cultural shift. Dave's chart suggests that two notions the Reformation did away with—myth and intuition—are now being rediscovered by postmodernity.

Friends of mine recently attended a "famine" weekend with their youth groups. The teaching was amazing, and working with the homeless was a powerful lesson, too. But the most powerful part of the weekend was doing **lectio divina** in an urban and poverty-stricken space that allowed for reflection, imagination, prayer, and, dare I say, intuition.
—**Holly Rankin Zaher**

The Enlightenment transformed both Christian theology and European culture. Over time, the modernistic approach to history and the natural sciences seemed to make a naïve belief in the Bible impossible, so in the nineteenth century liberalism rose to the challenge of modernizing Christianity. Biblical criticism drew on the new scientific method to examine Scripture. The Genesis account of creation was reinterpreted in light of Darwinism. Biblical critics questioned age-old notions about how biblical books were written, and who wrote them. Even Jesus became a subject for investigation, as scholars searched for the actual or "historical"

liberals in sheep's clothing?

Jesus that liberal scholars believed was obscured by New Testament writers who had a theological agenda that got in the way of historical accuracy as conceived today.

Conservative believers in all denominations reacted to what they saw as the liberal sellout to modernism with a powerful backlash. They were scandalized at the thought of subordinating the Word of God to what they saw as fallible scientific investigation. Early in the twentieth century one group of conservative Christians even made a name for themselves—fundamentalists—by defending the doctrines that they believed constituted the irreducible fundamentals of the Christian faith. These doctrines included the inerrancy of the Bible, the deity of Christ, the virgin birth, substitutionary atonement, the physical resurrection of Christ, and his bodily return to earth. In the following decades fundamentalists and liberals fought a bitter battle over who would gain the upper hand in popular culture, universities, theological institutions, and denominational bureaucracies.[3]

Although fundamentalists are evangelicals, over time it became clear that not all evangelicals wanted to be seen as fundamentalists. By the early 1950s, a group of respected scholars and a young evangelist named Billy Graham decided to distance themselves from fundamentalism, which they saw as anti-intellectual and overly defensive toward modern scholarship. They wanted to create a "new evangelical theology"[4] that wasn't fundamentalist but did affirm historic evangelical doctrines. Many evangelicals continue to hold a similar position. Indeed, thanks to negative media portrayals of fundamentalism and the regular use of that term to describe extremist elements in other faiths, hardly anyone now wants to be called a fundamentalist! But neither ideology—evangelicalism or liberalism—offers a fully satisfactory way forward for many post-evangelicals. Why is this so?

The Evangelical Option

Evangelicals have a deep love of and respect for the Scriptures. In my own case, I learned this love of Scripture from an evangelical heritage where, as a child, I was faithfully taught. Since then I have always been anxious to learn from Scripture. Evangelicals also have the acute expectation that God will speak to them through Scripture; that it is God's Word for them. Thus, for evangelicals, Scripture doesn't exist primarily to be dissected and analyzed. Scripture is a sacrament, God's means for communicating to us. Hopefully post-evangelicals will also always approach the Bible with a similar love and listening ear.

Evangelicals also believe that the heart of the gospel can be simply expressed while also challenging us on a personal level. This emphasis means that evangelicals have always been very effective witnesses to the gospel, and are responsible for the vast majority of conversions to Christianity. So, while post-evangelicals may well react to the oversimplification and, quite frankly, crassness of much evangelism, they shouldn't lose sight of the importance of presenting the gospel in a cogent manner to a world that still needs to hear it.

But there are also downsides to evangelicalism. Some, ironically enough, are even linked to the strengths just mentioned. Evangelicals tend to make an idol out of the Bible. I believe it was the Argentinean preacher Juan Carlos Ortiz who spoke of St. Evangelical worshiping a trinity of Father, Son, and Holy Scripture. This excessive exaltation of the Bible stems from evangelicalism's conflict with modernist biblical criticism in the late nineteenth century. While the Reformation also affirmed the uniqueness of Scripture—*sola Scriptura*—it did so in a different context—Catholicism's emphasis on the authority of church tradition rather than on Scripture's authority.**(f)**

> **(f)** I believe the main battleground is shifting for evangelicals. More and more are using the words Dave uses ("deep love of" and "respect for") when Scripture is concerned. Evangelicals are moving away from seeing Scripture as a battleground and to seeing it as a place where they meet God. They're moving away from understanding the Word of God as a defense for doctrinal truth and toward understanding it as a living, interactive dialogue with the God of the universe. Not only do evangelicals gain understanding about God through Scripture, they also encounter God in the Scriptures. Not only do evangelicals read about how Jesus' followers lived differently, they are empowered to live differently. More and more evangelicals are experiencing the Bible as a friend rather than a proof text.
> —**Mike Yaconelli**

Sadly, there's a huge gulf between evangelical scholarship and evangelical churches. Evangelical scholarship generally accepts the necessity of biblical criticism and utilizes its insights and methods. In evangelical churches, however, one will often find an anti-biblical criticism attitude. Evangelicals tend to bury their heads in the sand with slogans like, "The Bible says it, I believe it, that settles it." Go to your average evangelical church and suggest that we don't really know who wrote the fourth Gospel, or that the story of Jonah might be mythical, and you will quickly see what I mean.

liberals in sheep's clothing?

Closely related to this distrust of biblical criticism is a prevailing sense of certainty and absoluteness with respect to the evangelical understanding of just about anything. A dominant theme I encountered when talking to post-evangelicals while researching this book was their dismay at the lack of gray areas in evangelical churches. Virtually everything it taught in black or white terms. Preachers frequently denounce critical thinking as unbelief or a tool of the devil. This anti-critical credulity also shows up in the area of prayer. People thank God when prayers are "answered" and either forget their prayers or blame the devil when they go unanswered. I find it particularly irritating when someone says, "The Lord was really good to me on Monday..." I always want to respond, "Oh, and I suppose he was really awful to you on Tuesday and Wednesday?" Then there are the people who say things like, "So the Lord said to me . . ." Even with my best efforts to suspend my critical faculties, I cannot believe that God speaks to people in such clear-cut, matter-of-fact ways.**(g)**

> **(g)** Saying "the Lord was really good to me on Monday" could easily be another way of thanking God for some good things that happened during the day, and not a theological argument. Furthermore, just because God doesn't speak to everyone in this "clear-cut" way doesn't mean he never does. Consider the apostle Paul, Antony of the Desert, or Francis of Assisi. We ought to respect the spiritual experiences many evangelicals profess, even when they don't match our own.
> —**Mark Galli**

The Liberal Option

The irritation some feel with evangelicalism certainly provides them with an incentive to look at liberal Christianity. Many pick up books by liberal authors and find them stimulating. Given that they find evangelicalism too prepackaged and conservative, the openness of liberalism seems fresh and bracing.

I think it's fair to say, however, that liberalism has its own kind of fundamentalist problem. John Saxbee illustrates this by contrasting two distinct approaches to liberalism.[5] The first one, by S.W. Sykes, is what I'll call a liberal fundamentalist approach:

Liberalism in theology is that mood or cast of mind which is prepared to accept that some discovery of reason may count against the authority of a traditional affirmation in the body of Christian theology. One is a theological liberal if one allows autonomously functioning reason to supply arguments against traditional beliefs and if one's reformulation of Christian belief provides evidence that one has ceased to believe what has been traditionally believed by Christians.

Sykes defines his brand of liberalism in a very negative fashion. His liberalism has been influenced and shaped as much by its conflict with conservative Christianity as fundamentalism has been by its conflict with liberalism. He goes so far as to suggest that liberals should use reason to supply arguments *against* traditional beliefs.

John Habgood, who describes himself as a conservative liberal, comes across in a quite different way:

> ...for me [liberalism] represents an openness in the search for truth which I believe is profoundly necessary for the health of religion. We grow in knowledge, only insofar as we are prepared to criticize what we think and know already. True knowledge is tested knowledge, just as true faith has to be sifted with doubt... Openness in the search for truth also entails a positive, but again critical, approach to secular knowledge...It is essentially about honesty, but an honesty rooted in what God has given us, both in revelation and in the created world.

(h) One little-acknowledged attraction of liberalism for many believers is that it offers an escape from the harder edges of discipleship. When I was a pastor, I had more than one conversation with former fundamentalists who became Presbyterians so that they wouldn't feel guilty about not reading their Bibles or giving a tithe or whatever. These people were also not receptive to my preaching about the cost of discipleship.
—**Mark Galli**

Habgood's uses altogether different language than Sykes: words like *honesty*, *openness*, and *search for truth*. He takes a positive *yet critical* approach to secular knowledge. One need not agree with Habgood on many other issues in order to appreciate his method and attitude.**(h)**

Still, most post-evangelicals won't slide down the slippery slopes of liberalism, for at least two reasons. First, they are post-*evangelicals*. That is, their evangelical background still counts for quite a lot. Evangelicalism may prove frustrating in lots of ways, but it did help bring them to faith. Second, post-evangelicals also accept (perhaps critically) that the biblical accounts of Jesus are historical narratives. Unlike liberals

liberals in sheep's clothing?

who want to demythologize the Bible, post-evangelicals accept the supernatural nature of the gospel and the possibility of miracles. The Bible plays a normative part in their understanding of doctrine and practical Christian living, and they readily affirm the Apostles' Creed.

Two Sides of the Same Coin

Actually, both evangelicalism and liberalism are rooted in modernism, which is why post-evangelicals oriented to postmodernism don't feel comfortable with either option.(i) Evangelicals and liberals both accept the same basic "scientific" values for doing what both call "systematic" theology. The evangelical

> (i) In their lectures and books, many evangelicals offer a "solution" for the "problem" of postmodernity. But postmodernity isn't a problem; it's a culture. As any missionary can tell you, every culture is full of great opportunities for God to be revealed and areas that need God's redemption. When it comes to postmodernity, we need to ask "What, exactly, needs redemption?" and "Where is God already at work?" The goal is answering those two questions.
> —**Holly Rankin Zaher**

notion of inerrancy is based on the view that Scripture must have the same sort of accuracy in reporting past events that an objective modern history or science text possesses. This notion of scriptural inerrancy would have been unimaginable before the Enlightenment.

In order to accommodate critical reinterpretation of the Bible, evangelicals also increasingly oscillate between literal and non-literal interpretations. Far from being arbitrary, this oscillation is controlled by the need to defend the modernist presupposition that for the Bible to be "true" it must not contain any factual errors. With the increase of scientific knowledge that undermines traditional beliefs about the nature of the universe or evolution[6], evangelicals have shifted more and more of Scripture from the "literal" category to the "non-literal" one.

As we shall see in a moment, the objectivism of the scientific outlook is under serious assault. Objectivity is still a value, but the idea of objectivism—the belief that entirely objective knowledge *is accessible to us*—is disappearing. American theologian Walter Wink has mounted one of the fiercest theological attacks on objectivism.[7] After many years in the liberal academy, he took on a church pastorate. He discovered the enormous gulf between the sophistication of the academy and the actual needs of ordinary people. Wink became convinced of the need for a theology and a spiritual life which—while incorporating the fruits of the critical age—presses on to a more holistic consciousness than objective knowledge alone can achieve.[8] What he describes is actually postcritical or postmodern (some would say postliberal, but at this point, I am in serious danger of contracting post-itus!)—and I'm convinced this is where the future lies for post-evangelicals.

06

"let me tell you a story"

"let me tell you a story"

A new postmodern world is emerging as modernity, the enlightenment wordview, slowly crumbles.**(a)**

Postmodern people understand themselves using biological rather than mechanistic models.

Postmodern citizens see themselves as belonging to the environment, rather than over or apart from it.

Postmoderns are distrustful of institutions, hierarchies, centralized bureaucracies, and male-dominated organizations.

The postmodern world values networks and local grassroots activities over large-scale structures and grand designs.

It's where books are giving way to screens. People are hungry for spirituality, but dismissive of systematized religion.[1] In the postmodern world image and reality are so deeply intertwined that drawing a line between the two is difficult.[2] **(b)**

Those who assert that postmodernism is a figment of the academic imagination, merely a passing intellectual fad, could not be more wrong. Postmodernism flows directly from the musty corridors of academia into the world of popular culture. It's on the pages of youth magazines, in CD liner notes, and the fashion pages of *Vogue*.[3] It has abolished the old distinction between "high" and "low" art and created new art forms out of things such as music videos, urban graffiti, and computer graphics.

Few metaphors, in fact, sum up the postmodern situation better than *virtual reality*, for it is a world in which the old certainties are dissolving.

(a) There are times when the "evangelical" part of being post-evangelical still lingers. For Dave, this may be one of those places. The word "crumbling" suggests foundationalist imagery (i.e., a house built on the sand). It might be helpful for post-evangelicals to keep in mind that the modern understanding of truth—that it's constructed like a house on a rock—is imagery not worth using in a non-foundationalist age. Perhaps we would be more useful if we understood the world as transitioning, growing, becoming—not cracking and crumbling. Not only is it more endearing, it might be more accurate.
—**Doug Pagitt**

(b) What an incredibly exciting time to be alive as a disciple of Christ. The church has been pushed to the fringes of our culture and stripped of many of the props it has depended on for viability. Some view the move to the fringes as the end of the Constantinian worldview, where the church props up the culture to legitimize itself. Not being at the center of things has been cause for great consternation and upheaval within American evangelicalism. But while life on the fringes is scary, it's part of the church's heritage. Consider Israel's exile in Babylon, or the church before Constantine, during its first three centuries.
—**Timothy Keel**

the post-evangelical

(c) In their book **Cultural Creatives: How 50 Million People Are Changing the World**, Paul Ray and Sherry Ruth Anderson identify three demographic groups in America: the Modern, Traditional, and Cultural Creatives. Cultural Creatives, largely resistant to middle-class values, nevertheless define themselves by virtue of their own unique values. On their Web site, Ray and Anderson ask, "Does the religious right have a hammerlock on values in America?" They think not and go on to enumerate values that resonate with postmoderns and post-evangelicals. When evangelicals write off such people as New Agers, they're making a significant mistake.
—Timothy Keel

(d) Dave wisely suggests that post-evangelical churches are made up of postmoderns seeking to live the dreams and love of God in the way of Jesus. It's beautiful to see the many peoples of the world play in the kingdom fields of God. The issue isn't simply who we're trying to reach but who are we. The rise of post-evangelical churches is a result of postmodern, post-evangelical people expressing faith. At the same time most people don't use the categories in their self-understanding, and while it's helpful in these sorts of discussions, in real life people will have no idea what we are talking about. We need to be careful in the emerging church to not fall into the trap of defining the world in our terms and then providing answers to the questions we create.
—Doug Pagitt

(e) This is the Achilles' Heel for so much postmodern theory. Post-evangelicals seem to believe their claims are modest, but they really are sweeping. They claim they have no metanarrative of their own—but they do, one that posits postmodernism as the climax of history. They say, "There is no universal, objective truth," but they have their own version of universal truth—one that posits there is no objective, universal truth. Postmoderns try to clear the field of rivals by simply dismissing them to the dustbin of history or by defining them as out of order for wanting to talk about truth.
—Mark Galli

My thesis is quite simple. Culturally, post-evangelicals identify more closely with postmodernity than modernity**(c)** and this has a significant bearing on the way they approach and understand the Christian faith. One of the greatest challenges facing post-evangelicals is critiquing, and making a unique Christian contribution, to the new world they inhabit.**(d)**

A World of Different Stories

One of the most helpful ways of thinking about the distinction between modernity and post-modernity is to think of them as stories or narratives about reality. The modern or Enlightenment version of reality, which for a long time has been the "authorized" version, is a "big" story or epic that tries to explain everything. Modernity not only tells us how things are, but how they were and how they should be. Many different versions of the modernist story were written in nineteenth century, when it flourished. Darwin told the story of the evolution of species, Marx the story of social conflict, and Freud the story of the inner world of the human psyche. Altogether, these stories, or "meta-narratives" as they are sometimes called, are very appealing. Each story offers security via "once upon a time" beginnings and "happily ever after" endings. But what happens when the storyteller loses his thread? What happens when the

"let me tell you a story"

writer's hidden agenda begins to show? Or when we realize that these are *just* stories—perhaps convincing stories—but not reality itself? This is exactly what's happening in our world. The big stories and the storytellers are losing credibility. Fewer and fewer people today want to gather 'round to listen.[4] **(e,f)**

(f) Actually I think most people would settle for a good story. Part of the rub with post-evangelicals is that most evangelicals rely on apologetics to explain their faith. But apologetics can't satisfy the postmodern appetite for mystery, paradox, and imagination. People are desperate for myth, art, and story.
—**Timothy Keel**

This disillusionment with the great "epics" of modernity can be traced back to World War I, which, with its unspeakable horrors, shattered the dream that humans could grasp their own destiny and create a utopia using science. Add to this the Holocaust, the bombings of Hiroshima and Nagasaki and the famines and genocides and persecutions and ecological disasters that followed, and it's no wonder that the modernistic epic has run out of credible storylines.[5] As scientific and technological stories about progress lose credibility, the associated political and religious tales are proving less believable, too. What happens when the modern world loses its way? When dreams of "progress for the common good of humankind" turn into nightmares like Bosnia and Rwanda? Well, in the postmodernist world:

- people turn away from big stories to more modest "episodes." In other words, they are suspicious of large-scale explanations and universal moralities. Truth is whatever you find out for yourself, not a metanarrative someone else imposes on you.
- people distrust claims of certainty and objectivity; the world is a much more blatantly subjective place.
- we enter an age of pluralism and relativism. The unforgivable sin is to behave as though you have cornered the market on truth. The tendency is to "mix and match" stories from different sources and versions of truth, drawing on things new and old.
- the search for spirituality doesn't lead to conventional religion because religious metanarratives are no more appealing to them than modernist metanarratives.

Zygmunt Bauman describes this postmodern world as "modernity without illusions."[6] In other words, its claims are much more modest than modernity's; it no longer says, "Here is the truth—believe it!" It says, "Try this on for size."(g,h)

Postmodernity poses an entirely new interpretative situation for Christianity. The American theologian Walter Brueggemann suggests that the evangelical church in the West is unprepared for the task of reinterpreting its faith.[7] Why? Because evangelicals are lodged in a cultural time-warp, still interpreting their faith using the language of, and in the shadow of, the modernist "big story." This is understandable. Modernism has been evangelicalism's cultural setting for more than a hundred years. But it's time to move on.(i) Evangelicals can no longer assume that others believe there is an objective truth out there, somewhere. As Brueggemann says, all claims to reality are under negotiation, and theology can no longer make absolute claims in a vacuum and expect a ready acceptance.[8]

The Dawning of the New Age

The dark side of postmodernism is very dark. Bauman says it's marked by an "all-deriding, all-eroding, all-dissolving destructiveness."[9] Its ability to deconstruct all the old cer-

(g) The Anglican missionary Lesslie Newbigin concurs. He asks, "How can this strange story of God made man, of a crucified savior, of resurrection and new creation become credible for those whose entire mental training has conditioned them to believe that the real world is the world that can be satisfactorily explained and managed without the hypothesis of God? I know of only one clue to the answering of that question, only one real hermeneutic of the gospel: congregations that believe it." Over a couple of months a convert from atheism sent me a number of e-mails illustrating Newbigin's insight: "I know next to nothing about God or religion, but I do know that I have seen something so good about the way you and the people I met at your church care about each other. It has struck me that everyone is so kind and really seems to like each other! I have really wondered what could have made normal people act that way."
—Timothy Keel

(h) The beauty of what Dave is expressing plays its way out in many wonderful Christian communities. What he's suggesting is not a "take it only if you like it" attitude, but rather a "come and experience the story of God in the life of this community" invitation. It has been my experience in our community that the reality of God becomes something more than affirming mental assent to belief and is instead something to be lived. But lived modestly. The hope of the post-evangelical position is that it allows communities to be honest and accessible. Many of us from evangelical backgrounds know the sickening feeling of over-promised Christianity. The hope in the PE posture is that it promises what can be experienced, and for many postmoderns that is plenty. The call to live rightly in the world is much more attractive for postmoderns than the call to simply "believe right."
—Doug Pagitt

(i) I hope Dave isn't suggesting that at any point people will be free from cultural time warp. There are no culturally free people, and there is no culturally free Christianity. Among the many well-justified critiques of the entire "post" approach is that "they speak as if they will never make the mistakes of their predecessors." It is my opinion that we're prone not only to committing similar mistakes, but we also have the resources to take our mistake making to a whole new level! We need to be ever vigilant to not carry the seedlings of the "we will be able to get it right" attitude that seems to be planted in this comment.
—Doug Pagitt

"let me tell you a story"

tainties plunges us into a sea of confusion in which nothing is quite clear anymore. But Bauman also sees this process as a site-clearing operation, and he speaks of its potential to "re-enchant" all that modernity tried hard to "dis-enchant." What does he mean? Modernity, he says, was all about the declaration of reason's independence; rationalism and objectivism had to take precedence over everything else. It was nothing short of a "war against mystery and magic," he asserts, and in order for rationalism to win, "the world had to be de-spiritualized, de-animated, denied the capacity of the subject."(j)

In this scheme of things, the earth became a repository of "natural resources." We ended up with timber instead of forests and waterways instead of lakes. "It is against such a disenchanted world," Bauman says, "that the postmodern re-enchantment is aimed";[10] dignity can once again be returned to emotions, there is respect for ambiguity, and "mystery is no longer a barely tolerated alien, awaiting a deportation order." Now cold and calculating reason, not mystery or the emotions, is mistrusted.[11](k)

For those whose roots are in the culture of the big story, this process probably sounds either outrageous, or scary—or both. They wonder whether Christianity can abide postmodernity. (l)

Brueggemann, however, is quite sure Christianity can. He points out that postmoderns are actually more open to the spiritual realities and possibilities Christians profess. But Christians shouldn't promote their spiritual reality in absolutist terms. If we wish to take part in nego-

(j) For many post-evangelical communities, mystery is not the enemy to be concurred nor a problem to be solved, but rather, the partner with whom we dance—and dance we must. The call for the post-evangelical community is to dance and play the music. But we are also called to show each other the way into mystery. We would certainly be underproviding if we didn't offer new ways to enter and live in mystery.
—**Doug Pagitt**

(k) Modernity exalted the cognitive faculties and worshiped whatever could be mechanized. The sciences flourished in modernity. Perhaps post-modernity will reacquaint us with the "humanities"—the celebration of the organic, poetic, imaginative, and tragic. There is no limiting the power of the gospel, but I do believe it's better suited to dancing with the humanities than being dissected by the sciences.
—**Timothy Keel**

(l) There is an implicit change in the role and function of the pastor in the post-evangelical church. The time of the pastor finding her usefulness in being the "dispenser of God's truth" is in great transition. Soon the post-evangelical pastor will become **poet** (one who can put people's experiences into words), **interpreter** (one who can put people's lives into a greater context), and **guide** (one who can invite people into a communal journey). In many situations this will change the role and function of preaching from information exchange and motivation to an invitation into particular community practices.
—**Doug Pagitt**

the post-evangelical

tiating the future of our culture, we shouldn't act like privileged insiders who know the truth with certainty or allow ourselves to become "trivialized outsiders."[12]

The New Age movement is a classic example of the reenchantment Bauman describes and of the new openness to spirituality that Brueggemann writes about. Many evangelicals are nearly hysterical in their denunciation of New Age beliefs. In his book, *What Is the New Age Saying to the Church?* John Drane argues that the New Age movement represents an incredible opportunity for the church:

> simply because never before in modern times have so many people been aware of spiritual realities. Rapidly increasing numbers are finding it possible to believe in reincarnation, spirit guides, and extraterrestrials, and all sorts of other esoteric ideas. To traditional Christians, this might be unfamiliar territory. But it certainly means that these people are spiritually open as no other generation within living memory has been. All New Agers are winnable for Christ. In the case of every New Ager I have met, I've felt that God could give that person to the church as a gift, if only he or she could meet Christians in whose lives the reality of Christ was an everyday experience.[13] **(m,n)**

Without doubt, the scientific, materialist worldview that has dominated the West is collapsing, just as the atheistic materialism of the Eastern bloc countries has already collapsed. An exciting new era is dawning, an entirely new interpretative situation—but its challenge is not simply on the level of mission; it reaches deep into our own self-consciousness as Christians and human beings. The challenge of this new cultural reality goes deep to

(m) The call to engage in dialogue with New Age questions seems somewhat dated now. This should caution us about the need to "enter into constructive engagement" with every passing religious fad, as if each portends something significant in the culture. Test the spirits, as Paul says.
—**Mark Galli**

(n) There are many of us in the post-evangelical camp who are quite concerned that our communities don't simply become the hyper-individualized expressions of faith that marked much of the modern New Age movement. Post-evangelical Christianity might have much to learn from the New Age effort, but it should not be seen as the model.
—**Doug Pagitt**

(o) If only understanding world affairs was only this simple! This "collapsing" and "dawning" Dave speaks of is not nearly so cut and dry. There are plenty of cultures that have not experienced the industrial revolution, let alone the collapse of the scientific worldview. This issue need not be framed in one thing leaving and another coming. This issue is better understood as multiple worldviews existing simultaneously. We need not return to the attitude that in order for one way of thinking to be valuable the previous one needs to fail or end.
—**Doug Pagitt**

"let me tell you a story"

the foundations of our faith: the way we understand truth, the Bible, and even God. Postmodernity requires of us nothing less than "the deep interrogation of every breathing aspect of lived experience."[14](o)

Pieces of the Truth

In the past, evangelicals have sought to transform people by presenting the gospel within a whole, fixed, doctrinal, moral scheme expressed within a definite cultural form. I can illustrate this by comparing the evangelical gospel to a disassembled piece of furniture. When you open the box, you find a collection of various components, some instructions, and a picture of the finished piece. The instructions often leave you somewhat bewildered as to how to make all the pieces fit together so that none are left over. If you get everything exactly right, you'll have your piece of furniture.

Post-evangelicals, on the other hand, are more at ease with a box of components that can be constructed into several different pieces of furniture, some very basic and others highly elaborate. The instructions would even encourage you to branch out and imagine some other models of your own. This process isn't entirely relativistic, either, since there are restrictions on what can be made, since you only have a defined set of pieces that will fit together only in certain, well-understood ways. "Our responsibility," says Brue-ggeman, "is not a grand scheme or a coherent system, but the voicing of a lot of little pieces

(p) If Dave is correct, and I suspect he is, this will mean the end of the "mission statement, purpose driven" approach to community leadership. There won't be the acceptance of a single focus of a community of faith, no matter how snappy and easy it is to remember.
—**Doug Pagitt**

out of which people can put life together in fresh configurations."(p) We must make available "lots of disordered pieces that admit more than one large ordering."[15] This mirrors something Paul wrote the Galatians. Paul exhorted the Galatians not to fall for rigid legalism, but to stick with freedom in Christ, instead. The essential "pieces" the Galatians had to work with included the fruit of the Spirit (Galatians 5:22-23). They were to avoid mixing in "works of the flesh" (5:19-21). But otherwise their lives in Christ could be formed in a million configurations informed not only by their freedom in Christ, but also their God-given human potential and imagination.

the post-evangelical

(q) Global events over the last few years force us to recognize that postmodernism, while emerging, is not the outlook of the "world." This may be a new age, but its future is cloudy—not necessarily golden. Many cultures vigorously resist change. Many hierarchies have popular support. The good news of Jesus Christ can, potentially, be meaningfully told in any culture. Postmodernity offers us a hermeneutic of suspicion and finitude that should be helpful as we consider how to proclaim the gospel to these other cultures in these difficult times.
—Timothy Keel

(r) For those of us who chose the moniker of post-evangelical must be reminded that our way is not any more like Jesus than those who went before us. We are simply making an effort to be like Jesus in our setting. May God grant us the blessing of our forefathers.
—Doug Pagitt

If this sounds far too risky, Brueggemann assures us that the threat of remaining stuck in our rigid frameworks of certainty is far greater. I guess the problem is one of security. But the time has come for us to climb out of the little boat of our settled certainties and join Jesus in walking on the waters of uncertainty and vulnerability. As the German ecologist Rudolph Bahro says, "When the forms of an old culture are dying, the new culture is created by a few people who are not afraid to be insecure."[16] **(q,r)**

the truth,
the whole truth,
and something
quite like the
truth

the truth, the whole truth, and something quite like the truth

Thomas Kuhn, the philosopher of science who conceived the idea of paradigm shifts, tells of an experiment involving an altered pack of cards which contained anomalies like a red six of spades and a black four of hearts. Volunteer subjects were shown cards from the deck in rapid succession, including the strange ones, and asked to identify them. All the subjects got the strange cards wrong. As the exposure time lengthened the subjects became confused because they sensed the categories they had always used to place cards didn't fit these cards. As exposure time increased still more, most subjects realized why the cards didn't fit into the regular categories, and soon they were able to accurately identify all the cards. About ten percent of the subjects, however, could not make the necessary adjustments, even after the exposure time was increased to 40 times what most subjects needed. They became deeply distressed, and one exclaimed, "I can't make the suit out, whatever it is. It didn't even look like a card that time. I don't know what color it is now, or whether it's a spade or a heart. I'm not even sure now what a spade looks like."[1]

Kuhn came to see that research of any sort takes place within a paradigm, a whole cluster of beliefs and values that are taken for granted within a given community—like what sort of cards we expect to find in a deck of cards. A paradigm might also be thought of as a "school of thought." The paradigm determines which questions can be asked, what can (for better or worse) be taken for granted, and consequently, what the most promising lines of research might be. Paradigms function a bit like windows, which "frame" the reality you see beyond. When you look out a window, you're unlikely to ask specific questions about what the frame—or paradigm—doesn't allow you to see. **(a)**

Because paradigms are imperfect human constructions, and because no paradigm allows humans to see everything as it really is, paradigms are ill equipped to handle every anomaly or inconsistency. When too many anomalies rise, the community using the paradigm begins questioning its value, and the paradigm goes into crisis—with three possible outcomes. First, once tackled, the anomalies may be resolved satisfactorily from within the paradigm. Second, the anomalies

(a) It is this understanding that has reassured many post-evangelicals that the creation of transformative communities—not churches that focus on education and indoctrination—is where we ought to place our emphasis. Now we must struggle with "How do we then live?" The kind of conversation Dave is suggesting here requires a changing of the very approaches we are using. So, how do we do it? —**Doug Pagitt**

the post-evangelical

(b) For at least the last four centuries, theology's grand project has been the systemization of the Scriptures into an internally consistent interpretive grid. Sometimes exegetical gymnastics needed to sustain such complex grids doesn't do justice to the reality of Scripture's own variety. Post-evangelicals are more willing to preserve Scripture's tensions. They are suspicious of modern interpretive methods that attempt to explain too much. On this score post-evangelicals are ready to pursue Dave's third option.
—Timothy Keel

may not be solved, but since no alternative paradigm emerges that can do any better, the problems are simply put on the back burner; or third, the adoption of a new paradigm either resolves the anomalies or makes them irrelevant.**(b)** Often, the pressure of having too many issues on the back burner speeds the search for, and adoption of, a new paradigm.

One further point worth noting, says Kuhn, is that shifts to a new paradigm don't take place through straightforward logical development, but rather through inspired and imaginative leaps. The "conversion" from one paradigm to another involves a substantial intuitive element.[2] Obviously, this model of paradigm change, with its conversion moment, offers some interesting perspectives on the Christian life.

The playing cards experiment, which illustrates the difficulty people have dealing with anomalies, also describes what more and more evangelicals experience in their communities. At first they have vague feelings of discomfort about things such as the constant chorus singing or the dogmatic tone of sermons. Soon, bigger issues with evangelicalism crystallize, and the credibility of the paradigm is in serious jeopardy. Sadly, a few evangelicals react like the minority in the card experiments, becoming increasingly confused and stressed by the lack of satisfactory resolution. Frequently they either fall by the wayside or go through long periods of sadness or depression. Others bravely decide that their faith's survival may depend on finding a new perspective that makes better sense of it—post-evangelicalism.**(c)**

(c) It's important to note that the answer to this condition is not simply to change the "card" (the music or preaching style), but the change must come from the understanding of reality. For post-evangelicals it's not simply an issue of changing the packaging or method but the very understanding of the reality of God. This is why the creation of Christian communities is so important in the post-evangelical world.
—Doug Pagitt

"It's Not What You Know—It's the Way You Know It"

Post-evangelicals have found a different and, for them, a better "window" on reality. The most important change or "conversion" in this paradigm shift has to do with the nature of truth-epistemology. Post-evangelicals have moved away from the certainty that characterizes evangelicalism to a more provisional and symbolic understanding of truth. **(d)** For evangelicals, truth is rarely seen as problematic. Truth not expressed literally is usually not true at all. Post-evangelicals, on the other hand, feel uneasy with such a cut-and-dried approach and find themselves instinctively drawn toward a more relative understanding of truth.**(e)** Evangelicals usually interpret this sort of approach to truth as a sellout to secular or liberal forces. They object by saying things like, "But the Bible says…" or "We mustn't compromise God's standards" or "The truth is the truth, and we mustn't try to change it"—the assumption being that the "seeker" is deliberately playing fast and loose with what they know is right. From an epistemological perspective this isn't what's happening. The difference between the two paradigms isn't their opinions about what's true as much as a difference in the way opinions about truth are reached. Another difference between the two paradigms is their different language preferences: scientific or poetic.[3] Each language type presumes a distinct way of comprehending reality. The distinction could be expressed as follows:

> **(d)** I wonder if post-evangelicals are willing to concede that not everyone is called to wallow in the ambiguities of provisional truth. Evangelicals hold some truths with deep certainty and believe this certainty—faith—may even be a gift of God. Post-evangelicals may lack certainty as a divine reminder that the kingdom of heaven has not yet arrived and that our lives and theology are provisional until Christ comes again. But we need evangelicals to speak God's truth confidently in order to buoy up many people who would otherwise lead listless lives.
> **—Mark Galli**

> **(e)** I would go even further. Humans have a number of ways of knowing, and often these intuitive, relational paths inform how we exercise our will. We'd have a different world if Descartes had decided, "I believe therefore I am" or "we love therefore we are." If rationality is the only tool evangelicals have for discussing subjects of ultimate meaning, they won't connect with people outside their epistemological grid. Must postmoderns be converted to modern notions of truth in order to become disciples of Jesus Christ? Hopefully not.
> **—Timothy Keel**

Scientific Language	Poetic language
Precise	Imprecise
Permanent	Provisional
Absolute	Ambiguous
Propositional	Intuitive
Rational	Imaginative
Literal	Symbolic**(f)**

the post-evangelical

Naturally, in this context *scientific* and *poetic* do not refer to the field of science or the art of poetry, but to ways of describing and understanding reality. Scientific language aims to eliminate ambiguities by using precise and absolute statements. Poetic language delights in ambiguity and even plays with it, deliberately.

Evangelicalism frames its concept of truth using scientific language, and this has significantly affected how evangelicals treat the Bible. Naturally, evangelicalism also accommodates plenty of feelings, emotions, and intuitive insights. The whole nineteenth-century style of preaching the gospel, for example, which still strongly influences evangelistic presentations, leans heavily on emotional appeals. Charismatics say things like, "I just feel the Lord is saying..." and add prophecies and tongues and even laughing in the spirit to the mix. None of this, however, affects the absolutist fashion in which biblical truth is conceived. Even what might be called the premodern elements of evangelicalism is described in an absolutist, "scientific" manner. Take the emphasis on spiritual warfare, for instance. Descriptions of territorial spirits controlling towns and cities and accounts of "clearing the atmosphere" through prayer and praise marches all have a distinctly medieval ring to them. Participants, however, speak of such events in the rational, matter-of-fact way modern people speak about science, technology, or even vacuuming the bedroom.

Influenced by our culture's shift from a modern to postmodern mindset, post-evangelicals are less inclined to look for truth in propositional statements and old moral certitudes and more likely to seek it in symbols, ambiguities, and situational judgments.**(g)** This does not mean post-evangelicals are less passionate about truth than evangelicals. Actually, the opposite could be argued. When a community's truth is presumed to be a fixed certitude, people tend to take it for granted and fail to think it through for themselves. If, on the other hand, truth is seen as always being a step beyond our grasp, the need for people to think for themselves and engage in a persistent search becomes much stronger. My observations at Holy Joe's bear this out.**(h)** When visitors complain about the level of open-ended questioning they see taking place, I usually suggest that the questioners are searching for truth. Rather than take their faith for granted, questioners are honestly struggling for a faith they can believe in.

(h) The issue many post-evangelicals face is not simply concluding that evangelicalism has come up short in our own life experiences, but that the way of thinking that evangelicalism perpetuates is a holdover from the Protestant Reformation. And the realization that the world we now live in has outgrown the answers of the sixteenth century. The call of the post-evangelical is to do the work of the reformers and not to simply think like the reformers and recite them. Perhaps our need to study the past isn't for content but for clues on how to proceed and inspiration to continue on the journey.
—**Doug Pagitt**

"Anybody There?"
One of the most significant issues in the debate about truth concerns the interpretation of language. Deconstructionism—a postmodern method of linguistic criticism—questions the premise that language refers to real entities beyond itself. So, while we all understand the difficulties of communicating religious ideas and concepts to people outside our faith community, deconstructionists wonder whether there's anything out there at all.

Now, we should concede that a great deal of religious language is vacuous.**(i)** Phrases like "the Lord told me . . ." or "God is at work in the situation," or "the Devil's really been attacking me" are a standard part of many people's day-to-day vocabulary. However, after decoding, what such phrases really mean are something else, like, "I want you to listen to what I'm saying" or "Things are going well," or "Things are going badly." We are all

(i) While I've heard a lot of "meaningless God-talk"—and sometimes have been guilty of it—there is a danger here that all talk of God becomes suspect. Newbigin is helpful when he notes how we've elevated a certain kind of knowing (modern scientific rationalism) over other kinds of knowing, such as faith. Speech events are constitutive acts performed within the context of plausibility structures. Everything we say and hear shapes our perceptions of reality, a reality that exists within the framework of a community of people who share our outlook. Just as the university community, for example, has a plausibility structure that promotes a certain way of knowing and talking, so should the church. Unfortunately the church has struggled to find an equally compelling way to pass on faith.
—**Timothy Keel**

guilty of vacuous religious talk from time to time. The question posed by

the post-evangelical

deconstructionism, however, is much more basic. It asks how *any* of our talk, perhaps especially talk about God, makes sense.(j)

Don Cupitt, a radical theologian, says talk about God doesn't make sense. As he sees it, God-talk is little more than sophisticated fairy-tale language. In a reversal of one of Plato's stories, Cupitt asks us to imagine living in a cave from which there's no escape. All we can do is enlarge the cave, which is surrounded by impenetrable rock, as dark as night. We never go outside the cave, and nothing ever enters. We never see a dawn or feel a breeze. In the cave we tell each other stories about the life beyond in order to stave off the inevitable truth—there is nothing outside. All religious certainties come to us via language, Cupitt tells us, but the language is self-referential. The words do not refer to anything really outside. If you look up a word in the dictionary, you will simply be referred to other words; and when you look up those words, you are referred to still other words, and so on, until finally there are only words, he tells us, vast proliferating systems of signs. So it's useless to look for meaning outside language—it does not exist. All God-talk is a vain attempt to bring meaning into a situation that's ultimately meaningless.[4]

Of course Cupitt's chilling tale of nihilistic emptiness is itself just a story. Cupitt's tale is also not demanded of deconstructionist theory. Jacques Derrida, who considerably influenced Cupitt, denies that the nonrealist route is inevitable for deconstructionists. "I never cease to be surprised," he says, "by critics who see my work as a declaration that there is nothing beyond language, that we are imprisoned in language; it is in fact saying the exact opposite."[5] What deconstructionism does, however, is challenge the traditional assumptions that we can easily and accurately use language to refer to entities outside language. For the purposes of our discussion, deconstructionism does so in two ways: first, it shows us the all-pervasiveness of language—that we have no way of stepping outside language in order to prove something is objectively true.(k) Second, it shows us the immense difficulty of defining meaning unambiguously. The best we can do when we describe matters outside of language is use metaphors and models.

But that is not yet the end of the story. Another problem deconstructionist criticism has highlighted is that metaphorical language is also inherently contradictory. We will think about this point in a little more detail.

(k) How do we gain access to the truth? By God's revelation of himself, which comes to us via the words of Scripture. These words do not reveal the complete, exhaustive truth about God, but they do reveal sufficient truth for us to know God truly and do his will faithfully. These words reveal enough for us to live lives of certainty, joy, and fruitfulness for God. To desire more than this is to transgress the limits of our humanity.
—**Mark Galli**

The God Who Is There

Historically, metaphors have been understood as figures of speech, colorful ways of saying something that could be put more plainly. But metaphors are more complicated than this. They are essential to how we grasp reality; they express information that cannot necessarily be acquired or understood in any other way. At one level a metaphor is nonsense. To say, for example, that "time flies" is silly. Time does not have wings. Yet the idea of time flying fits our experience, too. For example, the metaphor might remind us of a time we were having fun but then suddenly realized how late it was; or it might remind us of how we were in a panic to get something done when time was "running out." For a metaphor like this to work, however, it has to have a tension at its very heart, a tension between its sense and nonsense. This tension can actually be located in the verb *to be*, which properly contains an "is/is not."[6] When say, for example, time flies, our audience understands that since this is a metaphor, what we mean is "time flies (and of course) it does not fly."**(l)**

(l) What lost or neglected metaphors can churches rediscover or reimagine that will help it reach out to postmoderns? Church as monastic community? Mission outpost? Artistic haven? Our metaphors will either free up or constrict how we conceive of ourselves; they will determine what we measure and value.
—**Timothy Keel**

But now, consider a metaphor like "God our father." Evangelicals tend to treat such metaphors in too literal a manner. For instance, they assume that saying God our father is a literal statement rather than a metaphor. Or when the Bible talks of God getting angry or rejoicing, evangelicals assume the Bible means God does so in a human or near-human way. In doing so, evangelicals abandon the ten-

the post-evangelical

sion inherent in metaphors. Consequently biblical metaphors cease to depict truth and sink to the level of crude descriptions of truth.(m)

Theologians have long understood the problems associated with attempts to describe God literally, using human knowledge. As far back as the fifth century, theologians tried to address the problem by allowing for two different ways of speaking about God: the *via negativa* and the *via positiva*. Traditionally, Christians have thought of the *via negativa* as the primary way to speak of God since it emphasizes the "otherness" of a transcendent God by suggestion that humans can only say what God is not. This perspective warns that anthropomorphisms (language which describe God in terms usually applied to human beings) are deceptions that are a kind of idolatry because they reduce God to a human image.

Once this method has established God's transcendence, however, theologians can also travel the *via positiva*, theology that makes affirmations about God's person. This kind of theology is based on the idea that God has revealed something real about himself in Scripture, creation, and in humanity in particular. The highest human qualities are therefore seen as pointers to God, even though they are not descriptions.[7] Karl Barth actually insisted that the only way we can speak of God is in a *via dialectica* or through an opposition of statement and counter-statement, of "yes" and "no," of paradox, in which the extremes of the negative and positive ways are held together in the response of faith. This way of looking at God emphasizes that God is beyond rational comprehension and, ultimately, dogmatic formulation.[8] This negative/positive tension in our theology of God parallels the metaphoric tension we noted and illustrates how poetic language is "more true" and more meaningful than "precise" or unambiguous scientific language that doesn't allow for metaphoric tension.

In summary, then, we can say that a theory such as deconstructionism helps us recognize three things about our God-talk:

• It's impossible to escape the constraints of language and objectively to say whether our beliefs are true or not. Whatever your choice, faith is required.

• Human language is unable to describe the external realities of God with any precision. As we have seen, this does not make language useless; it simply means that we have to accept its limitations.

• Religious language, or talk about God and the spiritual realm, is therefore inherently provisional and approximate.

Critical Realism Trumps the Naïve

One more perspective on how we talk about God might prove useful. Since Christians assume God is a real external being there are two roads they can travel down: that of *naïve realism* or that of critical realism. Naïve realism assumes that talking about God or the spiritual dimension in a literal or near-literal way is as unproblematic as our talk about everyday objects and experiences. This is the overwhelmingly dominant understanding in evangelical churches. For these evangelicals—if the Bible says God gets angry or rejoices, or if it tells us that he's a father or a king—then that is how it is. At the popular level, then, naïve realism corresponds to what we earlier called "scientific language." Naïve realism assumes that all expressions of truth must be precise, absolute, literal, and propositional. Thus, the Bible, as the ultimate repository of truth, must be entirely historically accurate. So, the argument goes, "If we can't believe that Jonah was swallowed by a fish, then how can we believe that Jesus rose from the dead?"

In her excellent book *Metaphor and Religious Language*, Janet Martin Soskice dismisses naïve realism, saying that it's the legacy of literalism that equates religious truth with historical facts:

Christianity is indeed a religion of the book, but now a book of this sort of fact: Its sacred texts are chronicles of experience, armories of metaphor, and purveyors of an interpretative tradition. The sacred literature thus both records experiences of the past and provides the descriptive language by which any new experience may be interpreted...All the metaphors which we use to speak to God arise from experiences of that which cannot be described, of that which Jews and Christians believe to be "He who is."[9]

the post-evangelical

I should stress that rejecting naïve realism doesn't mean one believes the Bible is devoid of historical content. However, it does mean that our faith need not hinge on everything in the Bible being historically factual.

Widely used in the context of scientific theory, *critical realism* affirms that many entities, though unobservable, are nevertheless real—electric, magnetic, and gravitational fields, for example. In a way these entities are transcendent, that is, beyond our direct observation. Thus, the only access we have to such entities is through the use of models or metaphors. When we speak of a gravitational field, we know that there is no actual "field," even though the metaphor does refer to an actual reality. What's more, this metaphor also informs us as to the nature of that reality. We could say that while such metaphors are not literally true, they do convey truth.

From this perspective we can understand a metaphor like "God the father" as having absolutely nothing to do with gender or biology. This metaphor discloses God's personhood and his nurture, love, and care for creation. How to understand this metaphor has, of course, been at the heart of the debate over women's ordination. Opponents to women's ordination claim that since God revealed himself in masculine form, and chose male priests in the Old Testament to represent him, women cannot properly represent him. But this argument leans too heavily on the "is" side of the metaphor and loses sight of the "is not" side. The "otherness" of God cannot be contained in either masculine or feminine images.

The Symbolism of the Cross

The Atonement is a subject area where critical realism can be put to good practice. Absolutely central to Christianity, the death of Christ is drenched in symbolism that draws on various Old Testament themes. Theologically, the Atonement has always been understood with the help of a variety of models. The vast majority of evangelicals understand the Atonement using the legal—also known as the substitutionary—model. It goes something like this: *Humankind is separated from God by sin. The only way his righteousness could be satisfied and our sins forgiven was through a legal sacrifice, without blemish, offered on our behalf. Jesus was that sacrifice, and through the shedding of his blood, we can now be cleansed and brought back to God.* **(n)**

Many people question this interpretation of Christ's death. Don Cupitt insists that the legal model of the Atonement makes God seem fickle, vengeful, and morally underhanded. Cupitt boldly announces that he was "taking leave" of this sort of God notion.[10] I know many Christians who've attempted to share their faith and faced similar accusations against God from those they tried to convert.

> (n) For many post-evangelicals who interact with the story of God as the running narrative in their lives, the notion of engaging in a theological debate around issues created by systematic theology not only has little interest, but also virtually no baring on their lives with Jesus. For those who choose a holistic understanding of the gospel story, the invitation to parse the language of reductionistic theological categories of ages past simply goes unanswered.
> —Doug Pagitt

From a critical realist point of view, the legal model for the Atonement becomes especially problematic. There are alternative interpretations of what happened on the cross. Consider one put forward by Stephen Ross White.[11] He asks what, exactly, did Christ's death achieve or change? The traditional reply of the legal model, taken literally rather than as a metaphor, is that sins were cancelled out, forgiveness granted, and therefore God's attitude toward us changes from wrath to mercy. White's version of the Atonement agrees that reconciliation was the goal but states that it was achieved through the demonstration of God's love, which *always* forgives, rather than through a once-for-all event of forgiveness.

What is changed, then, is not God's attitude toward us but our attitude toward him. The eternal love of God was shown most fully and graphically through his acceptance and forgiveness of the worst that human beings could hurl at him, the killing of his beloved son Jesus Christ.

In this way, the cross did not bring about forgiveness—this existed already. Rather Jesus *enacted* and *represented* the forgiveness that has always been in the heart of God. The Atonement is not about God's changing attitude toward us; instead the Atonement is about how our attitude toward God changes as we see forgiveness acted out before us. The evil we do is also annihilated in the light of Jesus' resurrection, and we thereby gain confidence to draw near to God in the knowledge that

the post-evangelical

(o) I find this perspective on the Atonement both personally and pastorally compelling. "Generation X" is the first generation to grow up in a post-Christian, postmodern America. Some sociologists also believe that Generation X is the most poorly parented generation of this century. Generation X knows upheaval and feels afloat. Generation X wants to reconnect to what has been lost or sacrificed in their lives. The relational (versus legal) conception of the atonement speaks to Generation X with warm, life-giving, hopeful language.
—**Timothy Keel**

(p) This interpretation of the Atonement (classically known as "moral atonement") has its uses, for it describes what often takes place in people's hearts when they hear about Christ's death. But we simply can't dodge biblical language that says something objective changed in the universe when Christ died, that sins formerly unforgiven can now be forgiven, that the chains of sin and death have been broken. These biblical metaphors consistently point to something that took place outside the human heart, even though it ends up transforming the human heart.
—**Mark Galli**

(q) Indeed the legal model begs many questions—and so does the moral model described here. What model doesn't? Here's the more important question: Are models biblical? One's model of Atonement shouldn't be determined by whether or not it feels good.
—**Mark Galli**

(r) Many in our community hold to the notion that the word truth needs very little help—and certainly doesn't need qualifiers like **objective** or **absolute**. How can truth be more than true?
—**Doug Pagitt**

he loves us and is able to transform our lives.**(o)**

This example offers a snapshot of how a critical realist approach can work. It may leave some questions: Is there, for example, enough of an element of sacrifice in Scripture to warrant the sacrificial symbolism of the legal metaphor for the Atonement? Does White's view of the Atonement exalt love at the cost of righteousness? Does it ultimately matter whether we respond to God's love?**(p)** But as we have already observed, the legal model begs many questions, too: Does God have such changeable emotions? Can he really be placated by spilled blood? How does one person's blood being spilled affect the status of billions of other people?**(q)**

"So, It's Just a Matter of Anything Goes?"

I recently led a discussion during which a student bemoaned the difficulty of convincing people about the "absolute truth of Christianity." However, if absolute truth is an attribute of God, and he is entirely "other" than ourselves, how could we ever gain access to such truth? Or, even if we thought we did have such access, how could we ever escape language's limitations so that we could test that truth in an objective way? Since language is inherently ambiguous in its attempts to describe all external, abstract realities, and therefore unable to express unequivocal truth, how can we refer to any truth as absolute? **(r)**

"Aha!" somebody says. "I knew it would come down to this. It doesn't matter what you believe. We can just make it up as we go along." Not at all. Why is it that as soon as we move away from the notion that truth always has to be absolute, we are told that the only option is to float completely free? I think the threat posed by absolutists is greater than the threat of "anything goes" posed by critical realists. Both extremes are deceptive. I'm certainly not advocating an end to objectivity as an ideal, but Walter Brueggemann is right to say, "The truth is that there is no answer in the back of the book to which there is assent, no final arbiter who will finally adjudicate rival claims"—not in this life anyway. And, as he goes on to say, most of those who want absolutes tend to accept authority only if that authority makes the absolute claims to which they are already disposed.[12] At this point we only have perspectives on ultimate truth and not ultimate truth itself.(s)

(s) Those unfamiliar with post-evangelical communities of faith shouldn't conclude that these are people of little passion or belief. They may be better described as a people who are captured by the story of God, not a people who have captured the truth of God.
—Doug Pagitt

When people assume you're floating free if you don't have absolute truth, they are making one very serious value judgment: that you are not seeking absolute truth. In his influential book, *Myths, Models and Paradigms*, Ian Barbour speaks of the tension critical realists must embrace:

• A combination of *faith* and *doubt*.

The "critical" element of this perspective recognizes the limitations of religious models. Doubt challenges dogmatism and questions the neat schemes in which we think we have truth wrapped up. Doubt creates a "holy insecurity." Faith, by definition, cannot be intellectual certainty or the absence of doubt. Instead, faith is always a trust and commitment despite the lack of infallible dogmas. Faith takes us beyond a detached scientific outlook to the sphere of personal involvement.

• A combination of *commitment* and *enquiry*.

Commitment does not rule out critical reflection, continued enquiry, or dedication to the search for truth beyond personal preference.

the post-evangelical

• A combination of *confession* and *self-criticism*.

Self-criticism admits that conceptual categories and human subjectivity limit our ability to formulate truth. At the same time, there are valid, helpful criteria for assessing religious beliefs.[13]

Obviously, much of what we've discussed in this chapter throws into question the way we treat the Bible, so we now need to address this subject more directly.**(t)**

104

is the bible the word of god?

is the bible the word of god?

I think it's fair to say that post-evangelicals have mixed feelings about the Bible. On one hand they have immense respect for the Bible and are keen to rediscover its relevance for their lives and world. On the other hand they have a backlog of negative feelings about the way they have seen the Bible used. Much of what others tell them the Bible teaches suggests it may oppose values they hold dear. Post-evangelicals also struggle with the "strangeness" of the biblical world compared to their own day-to-day reality.**(a)**

Evangelicals tend to assume that the Bible is the repository of absolute truth, that all you have to do to "get it" is read it—and do not take kindly to suggestions otherwise. Evangelicals accuse those who question their interpretations of Scripture, or their standard for what counts as biblical truth, with "going liberal" or "playing fast and loose" with God's word. Are they right? Can the Bible still be the Word of God for post-evangelicals, or has modern critical insight made that impossible?

> **(a)** Does it occur to anyone else these days that maybe we have things backward? We're so anxious to make the "strange world" of the Bible speak to the "real world" of today. Maybe it's our world today that's strange, and the biblical alternative is real, and it's the church's job to help people see that. In fact, this could be part of what it means to be transformed in mind.
> —**Mark Galli**

In this chapter I'll address these questions from the point of view of post-evangelical people who urgently need to find a fresh place for the Bible in their priorities, rather than from the perspective of conservative evangelical critics who are unlikely to agree with much of what I say. Too many people have abandoned Christianity due to unrealistic expectations with which they have been raised concerning the Bible. We need a new approach that affirms the Bible's credibility but also allows the Bible to speak prophetically into our situations. To find such an approach we must first attempt to transcend the polarized positions we often face in biblical studies.

Mr. Evans Meets Ms. Tomkins

Consider Jeffrey, a young boy attending Christian school. Jeffrey has two teachers, Mr. Evans and Ms. Tomkins, both of whom approach their tasks in bewilderingly different ways. Mr. Evans is an old-school Methodist and part-time preacher. Mr. Evans likes to say the Bible is his religion and his religion is the Bible. He believes the Bible in its most fundamental and literal sense. Jeffrey figures that if the Bible included Hobbits, Jedi Knights,

the post-evangelical

or Santa Claus, Mr. Evans would believe in them without question.

Ms. Tomkins, on the other hand, is a mainline Protestant. She believes the Christian faith must be reinterpreted for a modern audience, which for her means dismissing anything that sounds supernatural as "primitive" and "unscientific." She loves to demolish miracle stories. If on one day Mr. Evans tells the class the parting of the Red Sea was a divine miracle, Ms. Tomkins will tell them the next day that the parting of the waves was caused by winds and tides. Ms. Tomkins explains Lazurus' resurrection as a recovery from a cataleptic fit that made him seem dead when he really wasn't. She loves the word *psychosomatic* when talking about Jesus' healing miracles.

The whole thing came to a head when, in the course of a week, both teachers talked to Jeffrey's class about the feeding of the five thousand. Mr. Evans actually didn't have much to say. "It's a miracle, isn't it?" he asked. "JGoes to show that Jesus is God, and God can do what he likes."

"Miracle my foot!" said Ms. Tomkins the following week. "What *really* happened was that Jesus and the disciples shared out their own loaves and fishes with the people nearest them. Others, who also had some rations hidden away, decided to follow Jesus' wonderful example. Out came the sardine sandwiches they had been keeping to themselves, and of course there was more than enough to go around. The real miracle is that if only we share with others, the world will be a better place." That sounded edifying to Jeffrey, but it didn't strike him as particularly good news.

Over time, the conflict between Mr. Evans' literalism and Ms. Tomkins' liberalism resulted in Jeffrey acquiring a distinct dislike for the Bible and a feeling that only rather stupid people bothered with it. Years later he decided to take another look at the subject. Happily, he discovered an approach to the Bible that didn't require him to treat that Bible as simple history, ignoring all critical questions, as Mr. Evans had, and also didn't require following Ms. Tomkins in viewing the Bible as little more than a source book for moral fairytales. Today, Jeffery is an inspiring pastor and a theologian in his own right.**(b)**

(b) Naturally, these two portraits are caricatures to set up the post-evangelical middle way. But as the quoting of Karl Barth shows, this middle way is neither post-evangelical nor new; his middle way has been around for some 70 years. Mainline evangelicals have been studying the Bible while avoiding literal and liberal pitfalls for decades now. And they haven't all used Barth's neo-orthodox approach, either.
—Mark Galli

108

is the bible the word of god?

Many of us are familiar with Jeffrey's schoolboy dilemma. Many people who grew up in churches that took a literalistic approach to Scripture later find themselves unable to sidestep the nasty critical questions. Some are swamped with doubts about biblical credibility when exposed to scholarly studies during college, or when they start reading more serious literature on the Bible or theology. Others struggle with faith when they are engulfed by some personal crisis that confronts them with complex moral and ethical decisions. Sadly, many people never learn a more sensible approach to the Bible, as Jeffrey did; instead they give up on Christianity altogether.

The Inerrancy Debate—A Pointless Diversion

Some of the problems we face are not so much problems with the Bible as with claims people make for the Bible. Like many evangelicals I was brought up on the doctrine of biblical inerrancy. The crudest version of this doctrine holds that the Bible does not contain any errors at all—even when it speaks of history, science, moral behavior, or whatever. The argument is that if the Bible cannot be trusted on these issues, how can it be trusted at all?

Other evangelicals, like John Stott, the Anglican theologian, have a more moderate approach to inerrancy. He represents a strand of evangelicalism that seeks to deal honestly with modern scholarship. I believe fewer people would have turned their backs on Christianity had they benefited from his insight and wisdom. Stott dislikes the term "inerrancy," preferring to turn the negative into a positive by talking of the "trustworthiness" of Scripture instead. He understands the importance of recognizing different literary genres as an aid to interpretation. So, for example, Stott argues that poetic passages should not be judged on scientific grounds. Though he believes Adam and Eve were actual people, he sees no reason to maintain that the Genesis account of the Creation is a literal statement of how the world began.

Stott still is, however, an inerrentist—albeit a highly nuanced one. He qualifies his position in two ways. First, he says that only the original autographs (the actual manuscripts produced by the authors) are inerrant. Secondly, even then, these can only be thought of as inerrant when rightly interpreted.[1] Both points are rather academic since none of the original autographs exist, and in any case, who decides what is a

the post-evangelical

proper interpretation?

An even more fundamental problem with the doctrine of inerrancy, however, is that the Bible makes no such claim for itself. Indeed, the Bible says remarkably little about itself or the nature of its divine source:"One gets the impression that its chief task is to point away from itself to something or someone who is far more important."[2] Some passages affirm its divine inspiration (2 Timothy 3:16 and 2 Peter 1:20-21), but none suggests or implies inerrancy. Inerrancy is an ideology introduced into the text from outside.

James Barr, who has written extensively on the subject, argues forcefully that inerrancy is a (believing) rationalist response to (an unbelieving) rationalist threat. This view is rationalist, says Barr, in that it reasons Scripture cannot be inspired unless it's historically inerrant. Such a limited notion of inspiration is clearly linked to the imposition of a modernist worldview, which insists Scripture must be "scientific" language. And it doesn't allow for "poetic" language in or about Scripture.

At the end of the day, however, we must ask where these nuanced and complex arguments about inerrancy and inspiration actually take us. Passionate exchanges between those committed to the various positions don't address the only questions that truly matter: How does the Bible speak relevantly to us in today's world?**(c)** How can the "strange" world of the text throw light on the complexities of living in today's broken world? Unless these questions are answered, post-evangelicals are likely to become post-Christians.

(c) There are plenty of (propositional!) good arguments here as to why the Bible is not inerrant or propositionally authoritative, as well as good discussions on how it should be understood via symbol and story. But then why should we bother with the Bible at all? This is the question I've not heard answered well in post-evangelical circles.
—**Mark Galli**

An Honest Dialogue

We need to find a way to synthesize and transcend the different outlooks of Mr. Evans and Ms. Tomkins. We need illuminating interaction between the honest, critical questions of modern scholarship and the faith commitment of the believing community. All too often these two different worlds simply do not engage each other. They might connect at the local church level, but they seldom do. Clergy often shy away from the task, shielding congregations from difficult questions and cosseting them with reassuring certainties. We are left with a divide. Meanwhile, in

is the bible the word of god?

the confusion, many have pretty much given up trying to integrate bib-lical teaching into ordinary, everyday affairs.

In recent years, my own relationship with the Bible has taken the form of a conversation or dialogue. Due to my upbringing in the Brethren, I have always taken the Bible seriously. In my early Christian life it definitely functioned as a security blanket. I read it literally and thought of it as inerrant. Back then the idea of dialoguing with the Bible would have seemed absurd; one simply listened and obeyed. As the years passed, things became more complicated. I found myself ques-tioning many of the interpretations of the Bible I once took for granted. Even recognizing that they were *interpretations* rather than straight bib-lical truth was a breakthrough. But before long, I realized that every read-ing of the Bible involved an interpretation, and that taking Scripture seri-ously necessitated a constant dialogue between the text, the historical teachings of the Church, and my own thoughts and culturally condi-tioned presuppositions.

Most people who turned up at Holy Joe's over the years arrived with very little interest in the Bible. They were weary of having it pushed down their throats and demonstrated little, if any, faith that the Bible had anything useful to say to them. So we seldom started our discussions with a Bible reading. Eventually, I offered to set up a small group for any-one who wanted to revisit the Bible. Dubbed "A Rough Guide to the Bible," the sessions proved popular, and so we usually devoted some of the main Tuesday evening meeting time to Bible study.

The "Rough Guide" studies basically reflected the dialogical process just described. I would spend a session introducing participants to some of the scholarly insights and debates surrounding a biblical pas-sage, providing them with notes and photocopies of commentary mate-rials, etc. Then, over the next couple of weeks they would set aside some time to read the biblical texts and reflect on them. They also agreed to keep a journal in which they noted any questions that arose and wrote down their reactions to what they read. When we reconvened we pooled our thoughts and feelings about the passage. This time the emphasis moved away from the academic issues in favor of grappling with the sig-nificance and meaning of the text for today.

Methodologically, we were concentrating on literary and reader-response approaches. I believed if people could engage the texts (rather than an ideology about them) and enjoy the process, they might also engage with the word of God through the texts. The results were startling. People who had given up on the Bible started to read it again—and with the hope and expectation that it had something important and relevant to say.

The Bible as Word of God—In What Sense?
If I have conveyed the view that the inerrancy debate is a waste of time, that's pretty much how I see it. But I hope I have also communicated my high regard for Scripture and my firm belief that it can speak to post-evangelicals as word of God. I will now develop this line of argument by explaining how the Bible can be treated as God's word with the help of Karl Barth, who's sometimes been described as the first truly postmodern theologian.

Barth had a sophisticated understanding of the "word of God" as God's revelation. Not much interested in the inerrancy debate, Barth saw revelation as primarily personal rather than verbal and as the self-disclosure of God rather than a set of propositions. The word of God, said Barth, has a threefold form: the primary form is the *living Word* expressed in Jesus Christ; the secondary form is the *written word* of Scripture, which testifies to the living Word; and the third form is the *proclaimed word* which is the church's proclamation of Christ the living Word. The three are inextricably linked together, the Word of God in Christ being primary.

The Bible, said Barth, is not in itself revelation; instead it testifies to the revelation of God in Christ. "No one who reads the Bible carefully," he says, "will find in it any claim that its texts are, as such, a revelation of God." On the other hand, he continues, it's equally wrong to say (like the liberals) that the Bible merely includes the revelation of God. The whole Bible, he insists, is "pregnant with revelation."**(d)** Still, any search for an absolute and unconditional source of divine revelation in

(d) The idea that we can know the Bible like we can know the instruction book for my television is preposterous. To believe that we can march through all of its pages and capture its meaning and plumb all its depths with scholarly precision is to diminish and demean the Bible. As Parker Palmer so eloquently points out, "We do not know the Truth, it knows us." This way of knowing is at the heart of the postmodern view of truth. Truth is not something we corral or capture or tame. Truth is wild, mysterious, alive, and always on the prowl to capture, confront, and find us! The job of the seminary is not to explain the Bible but to strike terror into the heart of anyone who decides to read its pages. True scholars have not declawed the Bible. Quite the contrary. True scholars teach us to approach the Scriptures with deep respect. They usher us into its pages with awe and wonder, fear and excitement. The Bible is truly "pregnant with revelation."
—Mike Yaconelli

Scripture, Barth believed, inevitably faced the limitations of the biblical authors and the relativity of their time and culture.

Just as Christ is truly God and truly human, Barth also saw the Bible as both God's word and a human word. This does not imply that some parts are human and other parts are divine any more than some parts of Christ were human and some divine. The entire Bible is human word, subject to the strains, weaknesses, and errors of any human product, and therefore requires examination and study with all the critical methods available. Yet it is also divine word in that it has something to say which doesn't arise merely out of human thought or culture. Therefore it must also be studied with a listening ear, to hear what God will say through it.

Finally, Barth spoke of the Bible *becoming*, rather than *being*, the word of God. Barth thought it possible to read the Bible and even study it in a scholarly manner, and never hear God speak at all—just as one might have encountered Jesus and never seen beyond his humanity. The word of God in this sense is not a static quality of the Bible, but something that comes into being as God speaks through it in a living and dynamic way—why Barth says it is pregnant with revelation.[3](e)

(e) Barth's threefold understanding of the word of God contains some key insights and helps us think more clearly about a very important biblical phrase. But it remains true that Scripture contains words that are, in some sense, to be equated with the word of God. That is, the words of Scripture matter, not just the overall biblical story or the biblical metaphors. If we don't take these words seriously as words, within their grammatical context, we risk reading our own ideas into Scripture and fashioning God after our own image.
—**Mark Galli**

How Does the Bible Speak God's Word?

This framework, which suggests how the Bible can both be the word of God and a document with human limitations, provides the opportunity to ask *how* it speaks God's word. Sandra Schneiders, a Catholic theologian, offers invaluable insights in the critical realist vein described in the last chapter.[4]

"WORD OF GOD"—A METAPHOR

To say Scripture is the word of God is to employ a metaphor. God cannot be thought of as literally speaking words, since they are an entirely human phenomenon that could never prove adequate as a medium for the speech of an infinite God.**(f)**

Unfortunately, the only alternative to a literal understanding of this phrase, for many people, is to dismiss it as fanciful and untrue. But, as we saw in the previous chapter, this misses the whole point of metaphoric language, which is deliberately paradoxical, having at its heart an irresolvable tension between the "is" and the "is not" of the metaphor. To treat "word of God" literally resolves that tension by killing the metaphor. Then the "word of God" is reduced to a synonym for the Bible. Commenting on how such literalism is a "cancer of the religious imagination," Schneiders says that people who pursue it

> must regard each and every word of the Scriptures as equally and fully divine and thus absolutely true...The impasses to which this leads, the absurdity of the truth claims that must be made for patent human errors in the text, are too well known to require repetition.[5]

So what might the "is" of the metaphor refer to? We know in what way the Bible "is not" the word of God—it is a book of human documents—but in what way "is" it the word of God? I'd say the Bible is the word of God in that it is the symbolic location of divine revelation.

"WORD OF GOD"—A SYMBOLIC REVELATION
God does reveal himself through the literal meaning of verbal propositions, words and sentences, semantics or syntax, but through their symbolic meaning. The fact that the Bible is filled with propositions, and that we legitimately continue to struggle to formulate words that express divine truth, whether in creeds, systematic theology, or sermons, should not fool us into thinking these words are *in and of themselves* that truth. They are *symbols* of truth. We can and should study them, analyze them, meditate upon them, and absorb them—but we must not imagine that they *are* the truth.

is the bible the word of god?

It might help at this point if we say what we mean by a symbol. Schneiders gives four helpful pointers.

• Symbols are a vehicle of the presence of something or someone that cannot be encountered in any other way. Whether a symbol is a physical entity or a mental image, its essential job is to make something perceptible that is otherwise imperceptible.
• A symbol does not work in a vacuum, but only in interaction with the person who engages it. In itself the symbol remains lifeless, but once someone engages with it, it becomes active and can deliver its meaning—its revelatory powers are unleashed.
• Unlike a road sign, which is a separate entity standing for something other than itself, a symbol participates directly in the presence and power of that which it symbolizes. Rather than being something that has to be bypassed or overcome, it mediates the thing or person it symbolizes.
• Paradoxically, a symbol brings to expression something that it cannot fully express. Schneiders likens it to a pinpoint of starlight in a vast and otherwise darkened sky. In that background an unfathomable network of unseen stars and planetary systems exists. Since the symbol is but a minuscule manifestation of a vast background of "unsaid," it must always remain ambiguous and allusive, concealing, in fact, more than it reveals.[6]

Bear in mind that revelation, as we've discussed it, is not primarily about imparting facts, but the disclosure of a person. Revelation is the "divine self-gift which has been taking place from the moment of creation and will continue to the end of time."[7] While this divine "self-giving" reached its zenith in the Christ-event, God is pleased to continue revealing himself though Scripture's testimony to that event. Through the complex symbolism of narrative, its pictures and images, its parables and legends, its metaphors and analogies, and its plain propositional statements, the presence of God is powerfully and intelligently mediated. Our primary attention, and our faith-response to the Bible, is not merely to words, but to the One who is sacramentally revealed through the words. Being symbolic, however, the truth in the words must also be understood as ambiguous and in need of constant reinterpretation.

the post-evangelical

How Do We Hear God's Word?

The notion that everything can be explained exactly with words, that every object can be understood by the subject, is a distinctly Enlightenment perspective. Both liberals and evangelicals have tended, for different reasons, to fall into this trap. Liberals objectify Scripture because they believe the texts are only texts, simple words that invite modern scientific criticism. Evangelicals objectify the text by asserting that the Bible's words are literally God's words, and they must stand up to detailed scrutiny as to their accuracy. Understanding the word of God as symbolic revelation, however, leads the interpreter away from a subject–object relationship into a more intuitive involvement with the revelatory process.(g)

> (g) Actually, this desire to express things precisely in words goes way back—to the Bible itself. We see an early confession of faith in Philippians 2, for example. In the early church, it's the Apostles and then Nicene Creed. And on it goes. This is not a "reducing" of the faith. Language is God's gift to us, not exhaustive but sufficient to express the truths that need to be expressed to draw people to God, to prompt goodness, and to thwart destructive teaching (heresy).
> —Mark Galli

We have already noted that Scripture does not automatically become the living and dynamic word of God to the reader. Two key words—faith and imagination—explain how the word of God can come alive in spite of our limited human perspective.

"Take it on faith"

Most people think faith is a pretty unscientific, "an ungrounded persuasion" of the mind, as Locke put it. Michael Polanyi, an influential scientist and epistemologist, denies this assumption. In line with Isaiah's statement that, "If you will not believe, you will not understand," (7:9)[8] Polanyi insists all knowing is fiduciary—that is, based in some measure on trust or faith. Taking on Enlightenment objectivism, he says that we cannot know things from the outside; in order to know something we must "indwell" it, that is, "cease to handle things and become immersed in them."[9] Polyani argues that we must always begin with a faith-commitment, and so presuppositions are not to be seen as enemies of honest research but as basic essentials. But this faith element is not, in Polanyi's judgment, a matter of cold choice; it arises out of a kind of intuitive compulsion—call it a hunch—which provides the impetus for faith.

Polanyi also noted two vitally related aspects of scientific belief. The first is that when we adopt one way of looking at things, we auto-

is the bible the word of god?

matically exclude other ways of looking at them. Faith has a necessary exclusiveness about it. But second, if something is conceivable, it is also conceivably wrong. Consequently, faith-commitments are subject to rigorous self-criticism in order to distinguish between ultimate beliefs and subjective notions.[10] These two points suggest that at the very heart of faith there must be a dialectical tension between *commitment* and *doubt*. When this tension is maintained, no inherent contradiction between faith and reason need exist.**(h)**

It seems to me that far too often the initial "hunch" that leads people to believe in Christ and to discover his revelation through Scripture later turns into presumption and a sense of certainty that actually works against further growth. I believe this happens when the tension between commitment and doubt subsides or is completely abandoned. To lose the faith-commitment is to handle a mere book; to abandon the critical process is to commit intellectual suicide.

"Use your imagination"(i)

The imagination is essential to hearing God's word for two reasons. The first is that, as we have seen, revelation is essentially symbolic. Symbols operate at an intuitive, rather than a purely rational level, and imagination is the medium for intuition. The second reason is closely linked with this—faith itself operates on an intuitive and imaginative level.**(j)**

(h) The important issue for post-evangelicals is to not individualize our experiences with the Bible, but instead hear it and seek to live it in community—locally, globally, and historically. The failure of the modern understanding of the Bible is the belief that any one person can extract pure and clean belief from it.
—**Doug Pagitt**

(i) What is it about the imagination that's made it the enemy of some evangelicals? Why are many evangelicals afraid of imagination, afraid of meditation and contemplation? Where were they taught that the mind is a dangerous place, populated with demons and evil spirits ready to barge in on any imaginative thought? For decades this kind of thinking has robbed Christians of experiencing God through **lectio divina**, journaling, and meditation. Evangelical obsession with Bible study and theology has kept the majority of the church from interacting with Scripture, personally meeting God in Scripture, and becoming intimate with the words of Scripture. One amazing way to combat the busyness of our society and the worship of speed is through peace and solitude and quiet in the act of contemplating God's Word. This new generation of postmoderns wants more than words; they want to know what's beyond words. They are ready to accept that the Word of God is more than reading material, it's a way of living—an expression of the difference that knowing God makes.
—**Mike Yaconelli**

(j) There may be nothing more important to a post-evangelical understanding of the Bible than the use of imagination. This imaginative process must be done in community and is often heightened by the participation of artists. This sits in contrast to the reductionistic, scientific approach of modern evangelicalism. May we find the success in this effort that those who held a rationalistic understanding of the Bible found in theirs.
—**Doug Pagitt**

the post-evangelical

Polanyi, building on the revolutionary work of Einstein, re-moved the stigma from imagination and intuition (which continued to be present in much popular science), and restored their credibility as sources of knowledge. Imagination is, after all, a quintessential human act, and can challenge all our settled certitudes. Brueggemann describes it as the human capacity to picture, portray, receive, and practice the world in ways other than it appears to be at first glance when seen through a dominant, unexamined lens.[11] In other words, imagination is the ability to see the world as it might be rather than as it is. Imagination is the seedbed of transformation, and Scripture can become the treasure trove of God's word, out of which the imagination can be funded. Of the countless ways in which the imagination can and does mediate the word of God through Scripture, I can only mention a few.

Meditation. This is a form of mental reflection in which the mind moves back and forth through a particular passage, narrative, or character. Walter Wink[12] describes an especially useful form of meditation that combines Ignatian meditation with insights and techniques from psychotherapy. I've successfully used this with groups in which, for example, we've spent time thinking about the characters in the parable of the prodigal son. As participants imaginatively "indwelled" the characters, I've been fascinated to observe emerging insights and their transforming effects.

Contemplation. Contemplation tries to give expression to deep inner emotions of thankfulness, love, or trust toward God in a kind of mystic communion. Contemplation is less reflective and less concerned with fresh mental insights than meditation. Scripture might be used here during contemplation in a repetitive symbolic fashion, in which the meaning of the words subsides into a great sense of wholeness with the One who lies beyond them. Contemplation has the effect of turning off the mind's habitual way of perceiving the world, which is limiting, through repetitive rhythm. Taizé music, a rhythmic sung repetition of Scripture verses, can be a powerful aide for contemplation. If it is to remain Christian, contemplation needs to be funded by the great images and symbols of the Christian narrative. It can quite often be used as an extension of meditation.

is the bible the word of god?

Recitation and Storytelling. Hans-Ruedi Weber[13] argues that when the oral testimonies in Scripture were first written down, they were not intended for silent reading—they were meant to be read aloud. Literacy should not rob us of the enormous benefits of reading Scripture aloud! The skills of reading and telling stories have been swallowed up in the more directive and less allusive craft of writing texts. We need to rediscover those oral skills.

Art Therapy/Bible Meditation. Imagination is a way of breaking with words while still interacting with them. You may have sketched and drawn Bible stories at Sunday school, but have you tried anything similar as an adult? Using the methods and insights of art therapy, all kinds of good things can begin to happen as we portray the feelings and ideas emerging out of the symbolism of Scripture.

Bible Study. Our approach to studying the Bible needs to move away from the very directive style of an "expert" teaching the novice toward a more communal experience that heightens the imaginative process. I don't want to detract from the importance of scholarship and learning, but we need to find ways to make Bible study a communal exercise rather than a didactic oracle.

In his book *Experiments with Bible Study*, Hans-Ruedi Weber describes a whole battery of methods of imaginative study of Scripture. Much of the stimulus for his work arose from being challenged in 1953 to bring basic Christian instruction to a largely illiterate community of believers in a remote part of Indonesia. Overcoming his initial Western plan to "teach them to read and write," he engaged in a wonderful educational experiment instead. In his classroom "laboratory" he devised diverse forms of imaginative study, including everything from drama to storytelling, from clay modeling to role-play, from drawing to memory games.

Theological Study. The word of God can be imaginatively brought to life in the midst of the academic enterprise. C.S. Lewis spoke scathingly of much devotional study of Scripture, which he saw as frequently awash in sentimentalism. He spoke of loving nothing more than puzzling over a tough theological issue with a pencil in his hand and a pipe between his teeth. Yes!

To sum up, we can say that the Bible is God's word provided we recognize that the "word" is an event mediated by the Bible and not the book itself. Because of the dual human and divine nature of Scripture, we need to approach it both with all available critical skills, and with the imaginative faith through which we will experience God revealing himself. If post-evangelicals fail to approach Scripture in this composite manner, they will either slip back into the sense of certainty which so often dogs evangelicals or into the chilly wastes of liberal objectivism— or, worse still, into ex-Christianity.

09

positively
worldly

positively worldly

This world is not my home,
I'm just a-passing through;
My treasures are laid up
Somewhere beyond the blue
The Savior beckons me
From Heaven's open door,
And I can't feel at home
In this world any more.[1]

This song was the anthem of my early Christian experience. With its rough and ready sentimentalism, it pretty much sums up the piety and theology of my church upbringing. We believed that the only people who felt at home in this world were the unconverted and backsliders. For us, though, the world was enemy territory, a place full of temptations and pitfalls. Though we had no choice except to venture into the world on a day-to-day basis, the overall policy was "avoidance wherever possible." Growing up, I was told to flee temptation; urged to avoid places like cinemas, clubs, and bars. Friendships with unbelievers, except for evangelistic purposes, were discouraged (because such friends might fill your head with "worldly" thoughts). Friendships with unbelieving females were especially discouraged, lest they become unbelieving girlfriends. The rule of thumb was, "If you desire it, it's probably wrong!" I remember feeling guilty about my lurking desires to stay in this world for a while and enjoy some of its pleasures before advancing to the goody-goody pleasures of the world beyond.**(a)**

(a) This is a seminal issue in the post-evangelical distinction. Post-evangelical communities like ours define our following of Jesus not simply by right belief, but also in right life. It's our intention to be a blessing of God for the world. Our conviction is that the call of the church is to "download the intentions of God into the operating system of the world." For congregations like ours, there is no intention to be protected from the world, but rather to bring about the dreams and love of God in our world. This is in significant contrast to classic evangelicalism. It was Oswald Chambers, who—like many evangelicals who champion a personal experience with God over usefulness to the world—writes, "The great enemy of the Lord Jesus Christ today is the idea of practical work that has no basis in the New Testament, but comes from the systems of the world...The central point of the kingdom of Jesus Christ is personal relationship with him, not public usefulness to others." (**My Utmost for His Highest**, October 19) Many post-evangelicals simply disagree and seek to live useful lives in the way of Jesus and believe that you shouldn't separate the words you use from the life you live.
—**Doug Pagitt**

The Parallel Universe
Things have loosened up since then.
Going to the movies doesn't raise eyebrows. Reading the Sunday paper

isn't a sin. Even a beer or glass of wine passes scrutiny. Still, in much of evangelicalism, an underlying distrust of "the world" is still evident and fear of contamination is real. The contemporary evangelical response to this fear, however, is different. Instead of a host of legalistic prohibitions, evangelicals have created a Christian subculture that cleverly markets a host of sanitized imitations of what used to be the forbidden fruits of secular culture.

Evangelicals have created a cultural parallel universe: Christian festivals, Christian records, Christian holidays, Christian social events, Christian dating agencies, Christian theater, Christian comedy, Christian television, Christian aerobics set to Christian music—it seems like the resourcefulness of "Christian" imitation knows no bounds. I even saw an advertisement in a Christian magazine this week for Christian computer games. "Sick of Virtual Mayhem?" it read. "At last, a Christian alternative." What will we think of next? "Lara Croft Gets Saved"? "Church Plant in Sin City"?

This evangelical parallel culture doesn't just offer "Christian" substitutes for secular entertainment. Evangelicals engage in serious Christian social initiatives through a plethora of organizations. There are Christian schools, businesses, law practices, medical centers, and retirement homes. Many of these initiatives help meet vital needs. Ultimately, though, I wonder what really motivates this creation of a parallel, evangelical universe. Are we still afraid of contamination? Why don't we lend more support to the perfectly effective, "secular" institutions that already exist? Doesn't the parallel universe strategy betray a basic antipathy toward the world—a world that God loves?

Post-evangelicals want a relationship with the world as participant Christians. Post-evangelicals experience the "parallel universe" of evangelical alternatives as derivative, aesthetically second-rate, and escapist. They want to leave it behind and make their home in the real world. They have satisfying friendships with non-Christians. As one person told me, "I feel I'm supposed to have things in common with Christians, and generally I can't say I do; whereas with non-Christians I feel there are fewer expectations in the relationship." Post-evangelicals also look at secular culture more positively as a place where God is also graciously at work. In part, this is because they have a more hopeful view of the human condition than most evangelicals.

positively worldly

"A Bundle of Contradictions"

"Man is an embodied paradox, a bundle of contradictions."[2] The human creation process in Genesis exquisitely symbolizes this *paradox*. On one hand Adam was formed from the dust of the earth, while on the other he was made alive by the breath of God. Humans were created in the image of God.

Christian theologians have long speculated about what, exactly, the image of God means. Generally, they suggest that the *imago Dei* consisted of certain qualities in us, such as rationality, will, or responsibility. Usually, theologians point to possession of a soul as another unique human characteristic.[3] I prefer a more existential explanation of the image of God, like that of John Macquarrie. He argues that the *imago Dei* is best understood as the human capacity for "being." Unlike any other creature, human beings experience an openness in which they can move outward and upward.[4] That is, we can choose how to "actualize" ourselves to become fully human by making choices about our relationships to each other and God.**(b)** We can choose to grow spiritually, morally, and intellectually. The *imago Dei* is not a fixed "nature" but a capacity to "be" God-like.**(c)**

> **(b)** This business of "actualizing ourselves" (from Abraham Maslow) sounds vaguely Pelagian, and the talk of being "God-like" vaguely Mormon. I say so only to recall how such statements in other contexts have led to brutal legalism and oppressive works righteousness that post-evangelicals long to escape.
> —**Mark Galli**

> **(c)** For many post-evangelicals, a holistic view of humankind is very attractive, as opposed to the dualistic view encouraged here. Many evangelicals hold a Western-Greek view of God—God is "out there" and needs to be pursued—while many post-evangelicals find connection with an Eastern-Hebraic understanding that implies God can be found in people. This distinction influences how PEs experience God, pursue Christian faith, and view each other.
> —**Doug Pagitt**

The *contradictions* in the human condition lie in the fact that the image of God has been crippled by sin. The degree to which that image is, or is not, still present—both within the individual and within the collective human experience—is crucial to our subject, since our understanding of the world hinges on our understanding of the human condition. John Calvin took one of the gloomier views of this subject in his discussion of what he called the "total depravity of man." In his view, the image of God was completely effaced by sin. "Everything proceeding from the corrupt nature is damnable," Calvin said. Any apparent manifestations of "good nature" or virtue in unregenerate people is illusory and worthless.[5] Only God's "restraining grace" prevents the world from sinking into total disaster.

the post-evangelical

This assessment seems biblically questionable, extreme, and profoundly unhelpful. I would restate the meaning and effects of the Fall for the human situation. First, our present, broken, situation is self-inflicted. Second, the basic essence of sin is idolatry. In existential language, to sin is to turn from Being to beings and to seek meaning in the finite to the exclusion of the Infinite. Third, human fallenness is universal, and it also affects one's entire life. Finally, humans are incapable of reversing sin's effects apart from divine grace.**(d)**

Having said all this, we must swiftly add a couple of caveats. First, the image of God in humanity, though defaced, is not effaced. Even now, sin doesn't have the last word. Anyone can see this. All sorts of people, both Christians and others, are good, moral, loving, dedicated, creative, sacrificing, joyful, and so on. Though none of these qualities are, in themselves, redemptive of the human situation, they are all manifestations of God-likeness. Second, while humans cannot redeem themselves, this very helplessness evokes a search for the grace that can solve our predicament. As Macquarrie so aptly puts it, "If there is original sin, there is also original righteousness, if only in the form of longing for release and for fullness of existence."[6]

(d) Sin is not a theoretical issue for post-evangelicals. It is a very personal issue and a universal issue. The use of the old categories (this four-point description of the effects of sin) is not sufficient. In some ways Dave shows that to step beyond the overly simplistic theology handed to us is more difficult than it seems. I don't believe we need to clarify the effects of sin; we need to be about articulating a better understanding of sin altogether. Could it be that now is the time not only to look anew at our old categories, but also to develop new understandings of sin and salvation for our world?
—**Doug Pagitt**

I would be surprised if these comments create difficulty for most evangelicals. However, while they tend to agree that God's image is still present in humans, in practice evangelicals usually emphasize the falleness of unbelievers. This is important, because it bears on their posture to the secular world, motivating, for example, at different times, traditional fundamentalist separateness or, more recently, the evangelical push to create a parallel "Christian" cultural world safe from secular contamination.**(e)**

The traditional evangelical posture of looking down their noses at unbelievers, however, is far too simplistic and judgmental. If we accept that the quest for grace I mentioned earlier may be taking place long before someone believes or even considers believing in Christ; and if we accept that God grants his grace to those who seek, even though they know not what they seek, then our situation is far more complex than a crude Christian versus non-Christian analysis suggests. There is surely a significant difference between the *knowledge* of and the *presence* of God's grace. Some may have knowledge yet have little existential presence of grace, while others may have little knowledge of it yet a great deal of its existential presence.

> (e) Modernity has determined how we viewed sin and the image of God. Might an emerging culture give us new ways of looking at these matters? Most of the people I know will readily admit that something is badly screwed up in their lives. Many even use the term "sin." The abused and the abuser, the dealer and the user, the addicted and hurting—they all know about the power of sin. But do they know the power of God's goodness? Many who know they're sinners and have experienced evil at the hands of others have difficulty acknowledging that God's image resides in them.
> —**Holly Rankin Zaher**

C.S. Lewis makes a very similar point when he talks about heaven and hell as ways or "being," rather than as geographical locations. Instead of focusing on one particular decision as determinative of a person's destiny, Lewis portrays life as a long series of decisions or choices of "being"—choices of whether to be this or that sort of person. "Each of us, at each moment, is progressing to the one state or the other."[7] Adopting such a perspective significantly affects the way we relate to the world around us. Rather than looking at things territorially—the church as God's (therefore safe) territory, and the world as the Devil's (therefore dangerous) territory—or dealing with rigid categories ("church and world," or "Christian and secular," et cetera), we should see God at work in his world, revealing himself in all kinds of ways and responding to the inner yearnings and the faith-commitments of people everywhere. The world then ceases to be clear-cut, and we find ourselves dealing not only with the "bundle of contradictions" in the human situation, but also with the eternal Being who loves the world and is poured out for its sake.

A World of Difference
This brings us back to the practical question of how then we should relate to the world—its people and cultures? So far we have recognized the ambivalence of the human condition. Created in the image of God, we have also been stained by the Fall. The same is true of all human culture. It too bears both the imprint of God and the corruption of human sinfulness. But what exactly is culture?

According to one widely accepted definition, "The culture of a society is the way of life of its members; the collection of ideas and habits which they learn, share, and transmit from generation to generation."[8] Without a shared culture, members of a society would be unable to communicate and cooperate—or even know how to identify themselves. Culture determines how we think and feel, directs our actions and defines our outlook on life.[9] Cultural identity is an inescapable human reality.

Our entire concept of God is also conditioned by culture—both by other, often ancient, cultures, and our own. Such conditioning is inevitable, since the only way we have of conceptualizing God is through language—and language is cultural. For the same reason, the whole theological enterprise is, of necessity, a cultural exercise. If theology is to make any sense, it must not only use language, but it must use the language of its surrounding culture, which in turn affects what theology is saying and how it is understood. Theology must always be formulated and reformulated as cultural conditions change.

Again, as I've stated before, the provisional nature of truth in no way denies there's such a thing as objective truth and reality. It does, however, underline our inability to verbalize it or "possess" it. I sometimes think of "truth" as I might think of a person I'd really like to know. The more I get to know a person, the more I realize that absolute knowledge of him or her will forever escape me. So it is with truth.

Since culture is a human creation, it follows that it reflects both the human "paradox" and the "bundle of contradictions" we've already discussed. Culture is a paradoxical intermixture of the earthy and the transcendent; and culture betrays the awful contradiction between the divine and the sinful. All these factors are inescapably present in all human culture, "Christian" or not. To categorize a record, a novel, or a system of education as "Christian" or "non-Christian" (secular) is to judge such things only on their superficial merits—for example, whether or not they talk explicitly about Christian themes.

In reality, all cultural products are a blend of influences, and discerning which are most significant or dominant requires digging a lot deeper than labels. For instance, a "Christian" recording on an overtly "Christian" theme can still nevertheless be sexist, or arrogant, or intolerant, or materialistic. Christians sin, too. On the other hand, a "secular" recording may criticize or even ridicule some Christian value while also conveying humility about human potential or a passion for justice or gratitude for all things bright and beautiful. Non-Christians can be wise, do good, and experience God's grace. No culture is black and white; all culture is paradoxical and contradictory.

The Fingerprints of God

Post-evangelicals (as well as many staunch evangelicals) often bemoan the quality of cultural life in the church: "Christians always produce second-rate versions of what the secular world already does very well," someone said to me recently. But it would be wrong to imagine that this is just a matter of taste. Very often, secular artists, writers, or performers are actually wrestling with issues or celebrating life in deeper and more evocative ways than their Christian counterparts. Consequently, films, plays, books, music, dance, or even soap operas can often provide significant insights, moral reflections, or critiques of human relationships that stimulate one's spiritual life in a way that hardly doesn't often happen in the "Christian" alternative culture.

One reason secular culture tends to be more evocative and stimulating is the greater freedom non-Christians have to explore the full gamut of human emotion. Evangelicals suffer from a compulsion to avoid associating their faith with euphoric joy or dark emotions. As a result, people suffering from depression in these communities often feel guilty and condemned. But the matter is still more complicated. An enormous amount of creativity stems from the darker side of the human experience. In evangelical circles, however, this creativity tends to be stifled under a relentless tide of communal joy and triumphalism. Finally, evangelicals treat sexual matters and innuendo and erotic feelings as forbidden territory, too.**(f)**

Over the years, as I have aired these topics through lectures and sermons, I've found myself welcomed by relieved people who had

> **(f)** Because of the problems Dave cites here, the evangelical church has lost many artists in the modern age. Many were not invited to share their gifts or perhaps not welcomed at all. So now the evangelical church has to recover the arts, much like the church of the Reformation after its iconoclastic excesses. How will the evangelical church do it?
> —**Holly Rankin Zaher**

given up hope that their love of theater, films, or comedy would ever be affirmed as an integral part of their Christian experience rather than merely tolerated as something that properly belonged on the fringes of their life. These are not all young people, either. I remember a widow in her mid-60s who told me, "You don't know what a burden you have lifted from me tonight. I've enjoyed reading novels and going to the theater for years, and I have become weary of other Christians chiding me and telling me to do something more edifying with my time."

While this woman's experience will seem extreme to many readers, those of us who have tried to engage the church by introducing some secular culture into its life have found it a difficult task. When we decided to organize an arts festival, we thought long and hard about these things. Our dilemma was that we wanted to have an event at which we, the organizers, didn't have to apologize for our faith and yet which didn't function as a "Christian" event. We decided to include artists and speakers who didn't necessarily share our faith but who could contribute qualitatively to it. We hoped to attract an audience that cut across the Christian/non-Christian divide. In many ways it has been a modest venture that hasn't gone as far as we hoped. We've been disappointed by the negative response from many evangelicals, especially church leaders: "Was that band Christian?" "Did you know that rainbows are a symbol of the New Age?" "Was that speaker evangelical?" "How many people got saved?" Thankfully there's another side as well. Nonbelieving artists, speakers, and audience members have repeatedly said they could relate to this kind of Christianity. Many churchgoing people have said, "It's not like a Christian event—it's great!" Christian artists say they feel like they have come home at last.**(g)**

> **(g)** Post-evangelicals must be careful to not assume that it's the quality of art that makes it Christian. "Good" post-evangelical art may not significantly help the world. Post-evangelicals must suggest a new message, not simply a more effectively executed message. The issue Dave may be raising is the need for the church to be led by artists—not simply to benefit from their quality work.
> —**Doug Pagitt**

Of course, those resolved to be "positively worldly" face conspicuous pitfalls. The world, like the individual, is an ambivalent bundle of contradictions. Much secular culture is antagonistic to God and to the spirit of Christianity. Engagement requires discernment—not swallowing secularity whole. Many believe this is exactly what liberalism has done. In his apologetic for liberal Christianity, Donald Miller writes: "The danger in liberalism is that its Christian message may become a mirror reflection of the spirit of the age. This is an ever present problem for liberal Christians to confront...It is in losing the tension between Christ and culture that liberal Christianity has frequently lost its soul."[10] Yet Miller is right when he also argues that one cannot possibly criticize a culture without understanding it, and this is precisely where so much of evangelicalism has fallen down.

One cannot overemphasize the relevance of Miller's sound assessment to the post-evangelical situation. We have to find a way of engaging positively—even transform—our culture without giving in to its anti-Christian influences. I will finish this chapter with a few pointers for those who wish to follow this path of positive engagement.

To begin with, we need more *communal reflection* on issues raised by contemporary culture. On the whole, the evangelical church does not provide this. Forums such as Holy Joe's, where we enjoy open discussion or debate on cultural issues, can work in a variety of different settings: in homes, at the diner, over lunch at work. I will offer a few guidelines. Put some structure into the discussion. Don't make up themes on the run; decide on them ahead of time. Appoint an informal chairperson to keep the discussion on track. Finally, avoid the temptation to formulate a Christian "line" on issues; don't be afraid of open-ended conclusions.**(h)**

(h) I have facilitated a think-tank group that operated in this mode. It provided time and space that allowed for communal reflection. Using different Bible translations and art as resources was especially helpful. People wrote down provocative quotes and their questions and put them in a hat. Later we drew on these to get the discussion rolling. This prevented discussions dominated by one person.
—Holly Rankin Zaher

Second, both on the communal and the individual levels, we need to continually use the *biblical text* as the context for thinking about and discussing the issues raised. Don't try to apply the Bible in a textbook or rulebook style to contemporary issues. That usually leads to absurd, literalistic legalism or to dead-end frustration rooted in the fact that the Bible is an ancient, difficult text. Instead allow Scripture to *fund* deliberation, to act as a lens through which we view the contemporary world. At times the text will seem hopelessly remote from the real world. The temptation will be to stop wrestling with it and fall back on just our feelings or our mental deliberation to think issues through. This is a serious mistake.

Groups can help individuals overcome these difficulties. In a group different people think differently. Some people tackle issues pragmatically while others tend to think theologically or biblically. Each approach is a necessary complement to the other. The Bible seldom provides direct comment on contemporary cultural issues, but by grappling with such issues in the matrix of what Barth calls "the strange world" of

the post-evangelical

the Bible, we can find God's word emerging in a highly relevant fashion.**(i)**

Third, maintain *uncompromised integrity*. The conscience is a flawed and fallible apparatus, inevitably in a state of constant readjustment. We must nurture it. When Paul speaks about the different standards of his fellow Christians (e.g., choosing to eat or not eat meat or things offered to idols), he says "whatever is not of faith is sin" (Romans 14:23). He means it's probably more important that we're true to our convictions than whether or not our convictions were correct. We must not do things simply because others do them, nor force others to do things simply because we are happy about them.

Wherever we turn in God's world we find his fingerprints. Not just in the glories of the countryside, but also in the tangled web of human life and culture. With all the contradictions and ambiguities we encounter and experience in the world, we must never allow ourselves to forget that God is in the world, too, laughing, singing, shouting, whispering, healing, weeping, reconciling, enabling, resisting, and forgiving. God has not given up on it, and neither should we. I've long admired the writings of Michel Quoist, and especially his little classic *Prayers of Life*,[11] which portrays God involved with telephones, roller skates, glasses of beer, tractors, football matches, and delinquents. When he visited our arts festival a couple of years ago, smoking his pipe and charming audiences with his French accent and twinkling eyes, someone asked me, "How come a 72-year-old lifelong celibate priest knows so much about love, relationships, sexuality, and enjoying life?" The answer? He's positively worldly!

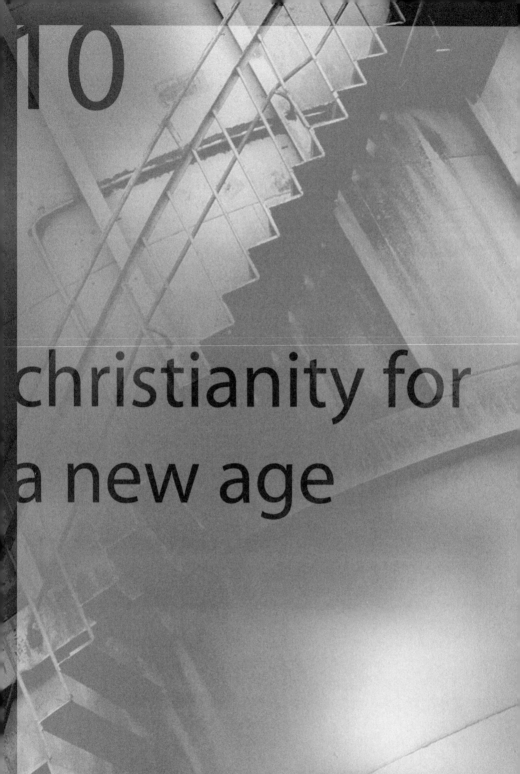

10

christianity for
a new age

christianity for a new age

A friend of mine recently asked a well-known evangelical leader if he'd heard of the term *post-evangelical*.

"Post-evangelical?" the man replied. "What is a post-evangelical? Surely, my boy, one either is an evangelical, or one is not an evangelical. Which is it?"

The plain fact of the matter, however, is that an increasing number of people see themselves as post-evangelical, and many more identify with what *post-evangelical* means without actually using the term. Something is happening here infinitely more significant than whether or not a bunch of evangelical "dropouts" can find a constructive way forward. My thesis has been that this bigger something is linked to a fundamental cultural shift underway in the Western world: a shift from the modern to the postmodern.

All churches in every tradition will need to take this shift into account if they want to continue to minister to this culture. Some evangelicals have responded to the shift by returning (in some cases with a vengeance) to the older certainties. In effect these people are saying that the only response to a sea of uncertainty is (try!) to reestablish the presence of absolute certainty. For many of us, however, this approach just won't do. We identify with those who are willing to engage more positively with the new situation and who also believe it has much to offer Christians, just as they have much to offer to it.

To some extent the comfort level one has with one or the other approach depends on the degree to which he or she actually lives in the world of the postmodern (or, as I would put it, the real) world or the degree to which one tries to avoid it. One of my friends said to me recently, "I can see that a lot of positive changes are taking place in evangelicalism, and I wish the people well. But the fact is, most of it has hardly anything at all to do with me or the world I live in."

Even more pointed are the words of the son of John V. Taylor, who, when he decided to give up on the church, apparently said to his father, "That man [the preacher] is saying all of the right things, but he isn't saying them to anybody. He doesn't know where I am, and it would never occur to him to ask!"[1]

As someone once said, "Whenever I hear people saying 'Christ is

the post-evangelical

(a) A church history professor of mine once recalled the seminary environment in the early 1970s. Some students were young conservatives fresh out of Bible college; others were hippies who came to Christ through the "Jesus movement." The professor described the cultural tension back then by saying one group knew all the right answers and none of the questions, while the other knew all the right questions but none of the answers. The people I pastor are similarly divided, although, on balance, more have thoughtful questions than easy answers. I want both groups to engage in open dialogue.
—**Timothy Keel**

(b) Relatively few white, upper-middle class intellectuals would identify with such statements. To be sure, those making such statements need to be reached, but let's not assume they speak for everyone in our culture. Or in other cultures, like those of Africa or Latin America or China.
—**Mark Galli**

(c) And how will we know the questions unless we listen? This type of listening does not occur during the typical church program. Post-evangelicals create space in their lives to listen to each other's stories and questions.
—**Holly Rankin Zaher**

(d) Evangelicals struggle to articulate a compelling theology of creation because most evangelical theology is subsumed into **soteriology**—the theology of salvation. Evangelicals want to know how to save people. This theological preoccupation, however, is passing away. Jason Clark, a pastor in the United Kingdom, observes that most of the issues to which the world wants answers relate to creation: ecology, gender roles, sexuality, and anthropology (which addresses a host of sub-issues, including "What does it mean to be human?" "When does life begin?" and "How do we deal with the powerless?" to name a few). Evangelicals focused on getting people into the next life don't have answers for such questions—and they should.
—**Timothy Keel**

the answer,' I always want to say, 'Have you the remotest idea what the question is?'"(a,b,c)

Let me summarize what I think are some of the key characteristics of this new postmodern world in which we live. It is a world in which people now reject truth claims that are expressed in the form of dogma or absolutes. It is a world in which dignity is granted to emotions and intuition, and where people are accustomed to communicating through words linked to images and symbols rather than merely through plain words or simple statements. It is a world in which people have come to feel a close affinity with the environment, and where there is a strong sense of global unity.(d) The postmodern world is one in which people are deeply suspicious of institutions, bureaucracies, and hierarchies. And perhaps most important of all, it's a world in which the spiritual dimension is once again talked about with eagerness and ease. Post-evangelical people, I think, are people who belong to, or are influenced by, this world and whose Christian faith is increasingly being expressed in and through this frame of reference.

Hunger for spirituality is all around us, and the selfish prosperity cult of the Thatcher and Reagan years has only deepened this hunger. In her book *Stare Back and Smile*, actress Joanna Lumley puts her finger on it: "More spirituality and less materialism are what we need in the West ... We're going to start finding our souls again."[2] My daughter Jeni speaks of the palpable attitude change she detects among her peers: In the early 1980s they were very skeptical of anything to do with spirituality, and talking about God was very difficult, but today her peers readily talk about spiritual things.

Unfortunately most people are not turning to the church to satisfy this hunger; instead many are turning to some expression of the New Age movement. Christians often see this as a straightforward rejection of God in favor of satanic deception, but is it? John Drane doesn't think so. He argues that the vast majority of New Agers are engaged in a serious search for God. "If anything," he says, "they are likely to be more open to a radical, life-changing encounter with Christ than are many Christians."[3]

Even where churches are turning the corner and growing, the majority of their growth is still coming from church transfers. So why is it that in an age of almost unparalleled interest in spirituality the church is still so incredibly unpopular to so many people? Keep these three important points in mind**(e)**:

> **(e)** Dave's estimate of church popularity makes more sense in his European context than in America. The church is popular in America, where weekly attendance at worship services has hung around 40 percent for decades, according to Gallup polls. The church is even more popular in parts of Africa and Latin America. Post-evangelicals would be better off admitting that for large numbers of people, the current church is adequately doing its job. Saying so doesn't mean there's no room or a vital need for post-evangelical ministry, but it would be a more realistic and humble estimate of their place in the larger scheme.
> —**Mark Galli**

1. The evangelical gospel tends to be much too "refined." In other words, it's a systematized *A-Z of Everything You Need to Know about Life, Death, and Eternity*—a modernistic "big story" approach to the Christian narrative. It's generally assumed that this "package" represents New Testament Christianity, and yet this sort of all-encompassing package is not what Jesus or the apostles taught. The prepackaged evangelical gospel is really their own construction out of a lot of little unconnected biblical pieces that—in their original contexts—were usually not part of a larger, evangelical sort of system. For example, the young ruler asked what he might do to inherit eternal life—a question that seems like it could function as a natural part of a larger evangelical design for evangelism. Yet Jesus told him to keep the commandments and sell all he had and give it to the poor (Luke 18:19-22). Not a very well-rounded gospel message! No mention of faith. No mention of salvation by grace and not works. Not even a mention of "making a prayer of commitment."

2. We need to take seriously Brueggemann's idea of "funding the postmodern imagination." He says that when we offer a full alternative world to people, we're acting in the imperialistic style that postmodern people in Scripture actually rejected. Rather than offering truth in the form of a dogmatic grand scheme, we must invite people to dream up their own biblically informed "fresh configuarations."[4]

3. In a similar vein, the usual approach to presenting the gospel assumes that "we've got it—you need it!" This take-it-or-leave-it approach is unlikely to cut any ice in today's world; the language of journey is more helpful. The world is not a place where Christians are over there on the right and non-Christians are on the left, with evangelism being the task of moving people from one side to the other. It's much more helpful to think of people as being on a spiritual journey where God is at work and waiting to be recognized. Evangelism should no longer function as a kind of religious sales operation, which often depersonalizes the individual being evangelized. Evangelism should be seen as opportunity to "fund" people's spiritual journeys, drawing on the highly relevant resources of "little pieces" of truth contained in the Christian narrative.

A recent survey found that 69 percent of Christians couldn't attach a date to their conversion. They experienced it as a gradual process, a journey. Soon after, I found a 25-year-old leaflet that turned the survey results upside down. Back then, 69 percent said their conversion was datable.[5] I am convinced that the cultural shift we've been discussing is a significant factor, if not *the* significant factor in this turnaround. John Finney, who conducted the former survey (which makes for very stimulating reading), says that those who evangelize often look for quick results, but in the light of this new trend, should pause to reflect. "The gradual process is the way in which the majority of people discover God," he says, "and the average time is about four years: models of evangelism which can help people along the pathway are needed."[6] The journey concept is apparently borne out by the facts.

Corresponding to the notion of recognizing the validity of others' journeys toward God is a willingness to admit to the ups and downs of our own journey. When Bono of U2 sang, "I still haven't found what I'm looking for," many evangelicals despaired, thinking he'd lost his way spiritually. Yet he was *quite* clear: *You broke the bonds, you loosed the chains, you carried the cross and my shame. You know I believe it. But I still haven't found what I'm looking for.* This is not a statement of confusion or spiritual ambivalence; quite the reverse. But it also recognizes the frailty of human experience and comprehension. We all know only in part, we experience only in part, and in a postmodern world, it's crucial that we're honest about this limitation.

Sadly, the organized church is the biggest stumbling block of all to the postmodern. "The uncomfortable truth," John Drane says, "is that the church has been all too eager to adopt the secular standards and practices of our prevailing Western culture." The result is that people see in the church a remnant of what they *see* and *reject* in the outside world: hierarchies, bureaucracies, and power struggles. And, as Drane says, "They know that this is not what will bring them personal, spiritual fulfillment."[7] This is not a time for churches to be working toward "bigger," "better," and "more powerful"; it's a time for the church to follow the example of its Lord and divest itself of its power, with all the personality jostling, political maneuverings, and empire-building that goes with it— the postmodern world is not impressed!

And Finally...

I said at the beginning of this book that I intended to do three things: Offer a degree of explanation of what's happening with regard to the emergence of the post-evangelical and why it's happening; offer encouragement to those who are thinking and feeling in a post-evangelical way—and wondering if they're alone in doing so; and offer some alternative possibilities for those who are clearer about where they've come from than where they're headed.**(f)** I would like to think that it will stimulate the necessary, rigorous debate as people wrestle with the issues of living as Christians in a postmodern world, and try to understand its full implications.

(f) How do we encourage each other during this cultural transition? Will post-evangelicals—even with insecurity—create a new culture?
—**Holly Rankin Zaher**

I can think of no better way to close than to quote again the German ecologist Rudolph Bahro: "When the forms of an old culture are dying, the new culture is created by a few people who are not afraid to be insecure."[8]

end notes

end notes

Introduction

1. Stephen Toulmin, *Cosmopolis: The Hidden Agenda of Modernity*, (The Free Press, New York, 1990), p. 203.
2. Maggi Dawn, "You have to change to stay the same," in *The Post-Evangelical Debate*, Triangle, London, 1997.
3. Dawn, "You have to change to stay the same," in *The Post-Evangelical Debate*, p. 36.
4. Mercer, N, *Third Way*, Vol. 18 No. 7, September 1995, p. 30.
5. Grath, A, "Prophets of Doubt," *Alpha*, August 1996, p. 28.
6. Richardson, J, *New Directions*, October 1995, p. 23.

Chapter 1: A Symbol of Hope

1. William Abraham, *The Divine Inspiration of Holy Scripture* (Oxford University Press, 1981), p. 113f.
2. Rowland Croucher, *Recent Trends Among Evangelicals* (Albertross Books, 1986), p.7.
3. John Drane, *What Is the New Age Saying to the Church?* (Marshall Pickering, 1991).
4. Ibid., p. 203.

Chapter 2: Just When We Thought We Had All the Answers...

1. Mark A. Noll, George M. Marsden, and Nathan O. Hatch, *The Search for Christian America* (Helmers and Howard Publishers, Inc., 1989). p. 78.
2. Ibid.
3. *The Atlantic Monthly*, October 2002, "The Next Christianity," by Philip Jenkins. p. 54.
4. Ibid, p. 1.
5. Dave Tomlinson, *The Post-Evangelical* (Society for Promoting Christian Knowledge, 1995).
6. Ibid.
7. Ibid.
8. Ibid.
9. Brian McLaren, *A New Kind of Christian* (Jossey-Bass, 2001).

10. Kennon L. Callahan, *The Future That Has Come: New Possibilities for Reaching and Growing the Grassroots* (Jossey-Bass, 2002).

Chapter 3: Worlds Apart

1. Kwame Bediako, "Biblical Christologies in the Context of African Traditional Religions," in Vinay Samuel and Chris Sugden (eds), *Sharing Jesus in the Two-Thirds World* (Eerdmans, 1983), p. 83.
2. Ibid., p. 89.
3. Tony Walter, *A Long Way from Home* (Paternoster, 1979), p. 159.
4. Ibid., p. 160.
5. Anne Borrowdale, *Reconstructing Family Values* (SPCK, 1994), p. 68.
6. Ibid., p. 69.
7. Adrian Thatcher, *Liberating Sex: A Christian Sexual Theology* (SPCK, 1993), p. 84.
8. Tony Walter, *A Long Way from Home* (Paternoster, 1979), p. 168.
9. George Marsden, *Fundamentalism and American Culture* (Oxford University Press, 1980), p. 35.
10. Tony Campolo interviewed in *21CC*, November 1990, p. 27.

Chapter 4: Longing to Grow

1. James W. Fowler, *Stages of Faith: The Psychology of Human Development and the Quest for Meaning* (Harper and Row, 1982).
2. M. Scott Peck, *The Different Drum* (Arrow Books, 1990) ch. ix.
3. E. Berne, *Games People Play* (Grove Press, 1964).
4. Thomas Harris, *I'm OK—You're OK* (Pan Books, 1973), p. 17.
5. John Barton, *People of the Book* (SPCK, 1988), p. 2.
6. Harry Blamires, *The Christian Mind* (SPCK, 1963), p. 50.

Chapter 5: Liberals in Sheep's Clothing?

1. Anthony Thiselton, *Two Horizons* (Paternoster Press, 1980), p. 14f.

end notes

2. Colin Brown, *Philosophy and the Christian Faith* (IVP, 1973), p. 50f.
3. A good account of this period is given in Marsden, *Fundamentalism*, pt. 1.
4. Millard Erickson, *The New Evangelical Theology* (London: Marshall, Morgan, and Stott, 1969), pp.30-45.
5. Sykes and Habgood in John Saxbee, *Liberal Evangelism: A Flexible Response to the Decade* (SPCK, 1994), p. 19.
6. John Stratton Hawley, *Fundamentalism and Gender* (Oxford University Press, 1994), p. 13f.
7. Walter Wink, *The Bible in Human Transformation* (Fortress Press, 1973).
8. Walter Wink, *Transforming Bible Study* (Mowbray, 1990), ch.1.

Chapter 6: "Let Me Tell You a Story"

1. Graham Cray, based on "From Here to Where—The Culture of the Nineties," unpublished paper, p. 5.
2. Angela McRobbie, "Postmodernism and Popular Culture," in Lisa Appignanesi (ed.), *Postmodernism* (Free Association Books, 1989), p. 170.
3. Ibid., p. 168.
4. Gerard Loughlin, "At the End of the World," in Andrew Walker (ed.) *Different Gospels* (SPCK, 1993), p. 208.
5. Hans Kung, *Global Responsibility* (SCM Press, 1990), pp. 2-6.
6. Zygmunt Bauman, *Postmodern Ethics* (Blackwell, 1993), p. 32.
7. Walter Brueggemann, *The Bible and Postmodern Imagination* (SCM Press, 1993), p. 1.
8. Ibid., p. 17.
9. Ibid.
10. Zygmunt Bauman, *Intimations of Postmodernity* (Routledge, 1993), p. xf.
11. Bauman, *Postmodern Ethics* (Blackwell, 1993), p. 33.
12. Brueggemann, *The Bible and Postmodern Imagination*, p. 20.
13. Drane, *What Is the New Age Saying to the Church?* (Marshall Pickering, 1991), p. 239.

14. Angela McRobbie, "Postmodernism and Popular Culture," in Lisa Appignanesi (ed.), *Postmodernism*, p. 167.
15. Brueggemann, *The Bible and Postmodern Imagination*, p. 20.
16. Rudolph Bahro, in Jonathan Porritt, *Seeing Green* (Blackwell, 1984), frontispiece.

Chapter 7: The Truth, the Whole Truth, and Something Quite Like the Truth

1. George Lindbeck, *The Nature of Doctrine* (SPCK, 1984), p. 8.
2. Ian Barbour, *Myths, Models, and Paradigms* (Harper and Row, 1974), p. 105.
3. Vanhoozer, Ricoeur's *Philosophy and Hermeneutics* (Cambridge University Press, 1990), pp. 57-61.
4. Don Cupitt, *The Time Being* (SCM Press, 1992), p. 33.
5. Stephen Ross White, *Don Cupitt and the Future of Christian Doctrine* (SCM Press, 1994), p. 198f.
6. This idea is explained very clearly in Sallie McFague, *Models of God* (SCM Press, 1987), ch. 2.
7. E.J. Tinsley, "Via Negativa" and "Via Positiva," in *A New Dictionary of Christian Theology* (SCM Press, 1983), p. 596f.
8. James Richmond, "Dialectical Theology," in *A New Dictionary*, p. 157f.
9. Janet Martin Soskice, *Metaphor and Religious Language* (Clarendon Press, 1985), p. 160.
10. White, *Don Cupitt and the Future of Christian Doctrine*, pp. 206-9.
11. Ibid., p.209f.
12. Brueggemann, *The Bible and Postmodern Imagination*, p.10.
13. Barbour, *Myths, Models, and Paradigms*, pp. 179-81.

Chapter 8: Is the Bible the Word of God?

1. David Edwards, *Essentials: A Liberal-Evangelical Dialogue* (Hodder and Stoughton, 1988), p. 101f.
2. Paul Achtemeier, *The Inspiration of Scripture: Problems and Proposals* (Westminster Press, 1980), p.106.

end notes

3. Karl Barth, *Against the Stream* (SCM Press, 1954), pp. 216-25.
4. Sandra Schneiders, *The Revelatory Text* (Harper and Collins, 1991), ch. 2.
5. Ibid., p.32f.
6. Ibid., p.35f.
7. Ibid., p. 39f.
8. Quoted in Thomas Torrance, "The Framework of Belief" in T. Torrance (ed.), *Belief in Science and in Christian Life* (Handsel Press, 1980), p. 4.
9. Michael Polanyi, *Personal Knowledge* (Harper and Row, 1964), p. 197.
10. Torrance, Belief in *Science and in Christian Life*, pp. 13-25.
11. Brueggemann, *The Bible and Postmodern Imagination*, p. 12f.
12. Wink, Bible Study.
13. Hans-Ruedi Weber, *Experiments with Bible Study* (WCC Publications, 1989).

Chapter 9: Positively Worldly

1. From "This World is Not My Home" in *Youth Praise* (Falcon for the Church Pastoral-Aid Society, 1968).
2. Charles Colton, *Lacon*, vol. 1, no. 408 (1820).
3. Andrew Linzey, *Christianity and the Rights of Animals* (SPCK, 1987), pp. 36-7 and passim.
4. John Macquarrie, *Principles of Christian Theology* (SCM Press, 1966), p. 213.
5. Ibid., p. 61.
6. Ibid., p. 245.
7. Michael Christensen, *C.S. Lewis on Scripture* (Hodder and Stoughton, 1979), p. 27.
8. M. Haralambos, *Sociology: Themes and Perspectives* (Bell and Hyman, 1986), p. 3.
9. Ibid., p. 3f.
10. Donald Miller, *The Case for Liberal Christianity* (SCM Press, 1981), p. 34.
11. Michel Quoist, *Prayers of Life* (Gill and Macmillan, 1963).

Chapter 10: Christianity for a New Age

1. Graham Cray, "From Here to Where: The Culture of the Nineties," unpublished paper, p. 13.
2. Drane, *What Is the New Age Saying to the Church?* p. 15.
3. Ibid., p. 213.
4. Brueggemann, *The Bible and Postmodern Imagination*, p. 20.
5. *Land Marc*, Spring 1993 (Marc Europe, 1993).
6. John Finney, *Finding Faith Today: How Does It Happen?* (BFBC, 1992), p. 24f.
7. Drane, *What Is the New Age Saying to the Church?* p. 236.
8. Porritt, *Seeing Green*, frontispiece.